# MAKE MORE WITH LESS

Foolproof recipes to make
your food go further

## KITTY COLES

Photography by Issy Croker

*Hardie Grant*

BOOKS

Published in 2024 by Hardie Grant Books

Hardie Grant Books (London)
5th & 6th Floors
52–54 Southwark Street
London SE1 1UN

hardiegrantbooks.com

British Library Cataloguing-in-Publication Data. A catalogue record
for this book is available from the British Library.

Make More With Less
978-178488-710-0

10 9 8 7 6 5 4 3 2

Publishing Director: Kajal Mistry
Commissioning Editor: Isabel Gonzalez-Prendergast
Copyeditor: Lucy Kingett
Food & Prop Stylist: Kitty Coles
Photographers: Issy Croker & Lizzie Mayson
Design & Illustration: Luke Bird
Production Controller: Martina Georgieva

Colour reproduction by p2d
Printed and bound in China by C&C Offset Printing Co., Ltd.

# CONTENTS

# INTRO-DUCTION

This book came from my want to show people that you don't need fancy ingredients, loads of time or a cupboard full of special equipment to make delicious food. That, and my belief that a Tupperware of yesterday's potatoes can make something even better today and that roasting a chicken isn't just the best way to cook chicken because it's delicious, but because it unlocks a week's worth of other, equally good meals, too.

I'm often so critical of the recipes I write. Because I work in food, I grew up around food (my parents had a restaurant for 25 years) and most of my friends work in food, I worry that everything I create has to be out there, innovative, new and amazing.

I have spent the last 10 years making cookbooks, and in that time I've followed and written A LOT of recipes. I've cooked everything from boiled calves' feet to fresh pasta and each and every recipe has been a learning curve. Being able to cook recipes from every part of the world is the best part of my job and I've learnt how to use the most obscure and amazing ingredients. But, what I've learnt most, is that people want to understand the basics first – the starter blocks; those few good methods or ingredients that, once you know them, will set you free in your own kitchen. Maybe it's because I do so much cooking that I've come to appreciate recipes that have few ingredients and steps – recipes that don't require me to trek over to that one shop in East London to find that one type of flour that you can only buy there.

So, I'm taking a step back from the more obscure ingredients to show you that you can make great food with ingredients you can find at your local small supermarket, or even with what's already in your house. I want to show you that those humble onions you've got lying around can make the most delicious pasta in 15 minutes and that the sad-looking bunch of herbs in your refrigerator drawer can make one of my favourite lunches in under 20 minutes. Flick through this book, then open your refrigerator or cupboard again, and I hope you'll say: 'I've got everything here to make that!'

This book isn't trying to reinvent the cooking world. It's here to remind you that sometimes the simplest things really are the best. It doesn't take a lot to eat and cook well, and I really hope I can show you how to do just that.

# HOW TO USE THIS BOOK

Before I started writing this book, I spent some time finding out what we all buy and waste most in our homes. I think everyone can probably guess the main culprits, which form the chapters in this book: jars, tins and pasta, potatoes and onions, eggs, vegetables, bread, milk, cheese and dairy, and fruit. I'm betting you've got every single one of those things in the house today.

Each chapter starts with a core recipe (these are marked with a coloured border and a grid of six images). This core recipe is followed by a handful of recipes that use that core recipe as a base (also marked with a coloured border). There are also recipes in each chapter that don't involve the core recipe, but instead riff on the main ingredient of the chapter, to help you use up any leftover ingredients.

This not only provides you with the basis for easy meals later in the week, but crucially cuts down on waste by using up what might otherwise wrongly be thought of as boring leftovers. My sister's boyfriend hates leftovers and that shocked me. It sparked a huge debate at the table, with each of us declaring our favourites ('But what about chicken stock? Bread and butter pudding! Christmas turkey sandwiches?'). The best things come from leftovers.

The reason I've included these core recipes is that I want you to be able to see how one recipe can be taken many ways – your own ways! Learn how to make and cook Meatballs (page 125), for example, then flavour and serve them however you want. A lot of us have been brought up to think that meatballs go with tomato sauce and pasta, but why wouldn't they be delicious dropped into a soup, eaten with a salad or scattered over some yoghurt and herbs with bread? Make a double batch (half for now and half for the freezer) and thank me later.

Béchamel Sauce (page 134) is one of the most basic recipes to learn, but it's the start of so many of our favourite things – Cauliflower Cheese (page 140), macaroni cheese (try my Creamy Corn Pasta on page 143 for an easy version), all different types of pastry- and potato-topped pies, croquetas, sauces, lasagne…

Bread is by far the most wasted food because of its shelf life, but please don't throw your stale bread away! So many of my recipes use breadcrumbs – and the breadcrumbs from most supermarkets just aren't good. It takes less than a minute to make your own, and you can dry them out or freeze them so they stay fresh. Please make the sweet sesame breadcrumbs on page 122, they are my favourite!

My versatile Green Sauce (page 62) is nothing revolutionary, but I wanted to show you how many ways it can be used. Eat a dollop with meatballs and mashed potato or stir it into pasta – very delicious!

The best way to use this book is to start by making some of the core recipes (I think the green sauce, aioli, meatballs and breadcrumbs are the most handy to have in the house for the week) and then from there you can freestyle as you wish. The opportunities are endless, and you can tailor the recipes to your personal taste. If you don't like parsley in the green sauce, just make it with basil! You can make these recipes your recipes.

# A NOTE ON INGREDIENTS

As someone who spends their life reading, writing and cooking from recipes, I still find it hard when there is a long ingredients list and a long method, so I've tried to keep as many recipes as possible under 10 ingredients and with quick and easy-to-follow instructions. The few things I'd like you to splash out on are a really good extra virgin olive oil, flaky sea salt, freshly ground black pepper, great meat and fish from your local butcher or fishmonger (the quality is so much better!) and, if not cooking your own beans from dried (page 15), then jarred beans. Apart from that, everything else can be run of the mill. Obviously the better the quality, the better things will taste, but get what you can afford.

## A few things I always have in the house that ensure a great meal

- A great extra virgin olive oil

- Chilli (hot pepper) flakes (I love Aleppo pepper)

- Flaky sea salt

- Fine salt

- Freshly ground black pepper (from a pepper grinder)

- Rice (I love sushi rice or short-grain brown rice, but basmati or jasmine are also great)

- Pasta (I love rigatoni and spaghetti as everyday pasta shapes)

- Good-quality tinned chopped or plum tomatoes

- Jarred pulses such as cannellini beans, chickpeas (garbanzo beans) or butter (lima) beans

- Good-quality sourdough bread

- Unwaxed lemons

- Garlic

- A selection of hardy herbs such as rosemary, thyme and sage that keep in the refrigerator for ages

- Onions (brown, white and red)

- Leafy greens such as kale, cavolo nero (lacinato kale), spinach or chard

- Some sort of hard cheese such as Parmesan, Manchego, pecorino or Cheddar

- Whole (full-fat) milk

# JARS,

# TINS

# AND

# PASTA

# BEANS FOR THE WEEK

Onion Butter Beans with Crispy Garlic and Pickled Chillies (page 27)

Beans with Artichokes (page 16)

My Perfect Bean and Tuna Lunch (page 23)

Grated Tomatoes and White Beans (page 24)

Broccoli and Parmesan Beans (page 19)

Pasta and Beans – The Comfort Bowl (page 21)

# BEANS FOR THE WEEK

Beans are having a moment and I couldn't be happier! I spent a lot of time in Spain as a child and beans are big there, so I could talk endlessly about how amazingly versatile they are, but I'll leave that to Bold Bean Co to do (they sell delicious beans and have a have a whole book about them).

This recipe is about making beans, but it's also about buying them, too. Most people I know who work in food will agree, buy jarred! The difference between jarred and tinned beans is huge. The taste, the texture, the lot. That being said, jarred beans can be expensive. So my next recommendation is to cook them from dried! I've made a big batch in the recipe below, but feel free to halve it.

**Serves 4–6, or enough for 3 meals for 2 people**

450 g (1 lb) dried beans or other legumes, such as chickpeas (garbanzo beans), cannellini beans, pinto beans, butter (lima) beans or haricot (navy) beans
any combination of vegetables, such as onion, garlic, carrot, fennel, celery
any combination of herbs and aromatics, such as parsley, thyme, bay, rosemary, oregano, dried chillies, fennel seeds, coriander seeds
water, to cover
sea salt

**Optional extras**
4–6 sundried tomatoes
2 vine tomatoes
1 vegetable or chicken stock cube
3 cm (1¼ inch) piece of fresh ginger root, sliced
bunch of spring onions (scallions) (or the ends of a bunch you have leftover)

Soak chosen beans in plenty of water for 12-24 hours, topping up the water as they soak. Give the beans a rinse, then transfer them to a large saucepan with your chosen vegetables, herbs, aromatics and any optional extras, a pinch of salt and enough water to cover everything by at least 10 cm (4 inches), as the beans will expand during cooking.

Bring to the boil, then reduce to a simmer and cook for 1–2 hours until the beans are soft and creamy. Remove from the heat and scoop out the extras, leaving just the beans and the liquid, then allow to cool.

Transfer to a jar and refrigerate until needed. They will last for a week in the refrigerator, ready to be used in different things during the week – I've included a few ideas over the following pages.

# Beans with Artichokes

A bowl of these beans feels so comforting and indulgent, but really, they are super healthy and easy, making them a great midweek dinner. They can also be made vegan by leaving out the Parmesan, or bacon lardons can be added for a bit of extra depth and heft. There's something quite Roman about this recipe – maybe it's the artichokes, or maybe it's the beans' simple beigeness. I've made these as a side to roast chicken (page 90) with a big bowl of steamed greens and I highly recommend it.

I sound like everyone else when I say this, but if you're using shop-bought beans, get the good ones – the jarred ones – if you can. The taste and texture is so much better.

**Serves 2, or 4 as a side**

2 tablespoons olive oil
1 onion, finely chopped
1 garlic clove, grated
600 g (1 lb 5 oz) Beans for the
    Week (page 15) or 1 x
    400 g (14 oz) tin/600 g (1 lb 5
    oz) jar of white beans
75 ml (2½ fl oz/5 tablespoons)
    water (if using tinned beans)
1 x 200 g (7 oz) jar or tin of
    artichoke hearts, drained
50 g (1¾ oz) Parmesan, grated,
    plus extra to serve
juice of ½ lemon, plus zest
    to serve
1 tablespoon extra virgin olive oil
sea salt and freshly ground
    black pepper

Heat the olive oil in a saucepan over a medium heat and fry the onion for about 8 minutes until very, very soft. Be patient here, this is the key to the dish and if the onion is done properly, everything will taste good.

Once the onion is looking delicious, add the garlic and cook for a further minute, then add the beans. If you're using the Beans for the Week or jarred beans, add them to the onions with all their juices and gently warm them through, stirring gently. If you're using tinned beans, drain them and add them with the water, then bring to the boil and simmer for 5–7 minutes until soft.

Add the artichokes and the grated Parmesan, along with the lemon juice and a very generous amount of black pepper and a pinch of salt, then taste and adjust the seasoning if needed.

Spoon onto a platter or into bowls and serve with an extra sprinkle of Parmesan, a drizzle of extra virgin olive oil and a little lemon zest.

# Broccoli and Parmesan Beans

There's a famous Italian pasta recipe that's made with lots of soft, cooked-down broccoli and it's the most basic pasta recipe but one of my favourites. Here, I've made something similar but with beans instead of pasta, because I love that the juice from the beans creates a thick sauce with the Parmesan. Think cacio e pepe beans with broccoli. Best eaten in a bowl on your lap while watching TV.

**Serves 2**

1 broccoli, florets and stalk, cut into 2 cm (¾ inch) chunks
3 tablespoons extra virgin olive oil, plus extra to serve
1 garlic clove, thinly sliced
pinch of chilli (hot pepper) flakes (optional)
600 g (1 lb 5 oz) Beans for the Week (page 15) or 1x 400 g (14 oz) tin/600 g (1 lb 5 oz) jar of beans of choice, such as cannellini beans
75 ml (2½ fl oz/5 tablespoons) water (if using tinned beans)
juice of ½ lemon
small handful of parsley leaves, finely chopped
20–30 g (¾–1 oz) Parmesan, grated, plus extra to serve
sea salt and freshly ground black pepper

Cook the broccoli stalks in a saucepan of salted boiling water for 3 minutes, then add the florets and cook both for a further 4 minutes until completely cooked through.

Heat the olive oil a wide frying pan (skillet) or saucepan over a medium heat and fry the garlic with a pinch of salt and the chilli flakes, if using, for 2 minutes until the garlic is softened and a little golden.

Add the drained broccoli with a splash of water, then simmer for 2 minutes until the broccoli starts to break down. Slightly mash the broccoli with the back of a fork, leaving some chunkier bits, then add the beans. If you're using the beans for the week or jarred beans, add them to the broccoli with all their juices and gently warm them through, stirring gently. If you're using tinned beans, drain them and add them with the water, then bring to the boil and simmer for 5–7 minutes until soft. Stir in the lemon juice and the parsley.

Allow to bubble for 3 minutes before adding the grated Parmesan and plenty of black pepper.

Serve with an extra drizzle of extra virgin olive oil and more Parmesan.

# Pasta and Beans – The Comfort Bowl

I think this is an all-year-round one-pot meal that makes the most of your store cupboard. It's a classic Italian dish made in various ways and I love it every time. You can bulk it out by frying off finely chopped onions, celery and carrots at the start with the garlic until soft for a more veg-packed version. I also throw in a handful of shredded seasonal greens at the end to wilt, such as spinach, cavolo nero (lacinato kale) or kale. Use any pasta or bean type you have!

**Serves 4**

3 tablespoons extra virgin olive oil
2 garlic cloves, finely sliced
1 sprig of rosemary or thyme,
  leaves picked
pinch of chilli (hot pepper) flakes
2 tablespoons tomato purée
  (paste)
1 x 400 g (14 oz) tin of beans,
  such as cannellini, chickpeas
  (garbanzo beans) or butter
  (lima) beans or 400 g (14 oz)
  Beans for the Week (page 15)
1 litre (34 fl oz/4¼ cups) bean
  cooking/tin liquid and chicken
  or vegetable stock
200 g (7 oz) pasta, such as
  casarecce, macaroni or rigatoni
50 g (1¾ oz) pecorino or
  Parmesan, finely grated
sea salt and freshly ground
  black pepper

**For the flavoured oil topping**
6 tablespoons extra virgin olive oil
3 garlic cloves, very thinly sliced
2 sprigs of rosemary, stems
  removed
pinch of chilli (hot pepper) flakes
juice of ½ lemon

In a large saucepan, heat the olive oil over a medium heat and add the garlic and rosemary before the oil is hot to prevent the herbs burning. Season with a pinch of salt and cook, stirring frequently, for 2 minutes until the garlic softens and turns very lightly golden. Add the chilli flakes and tomato puree, then continue to cook, stirring constantly, until fragrant and the tomato puree turns a dark red.

Add one-quarter of the beans with the liquid from the jar or tin (or 150 ml/5 fl oz/scant ⅔ cup of liquid if using beans for the week). Then, with the back of a fork or masher, crush the beans until completely broken down, this will create the creamy texture you want for the sauce. Now add the remaining beans, plus the bean liquid and stock mixture, then season with black pepper and a pinch of salt.

Bring to the boil over a medium-high heat, then stir in the pasta and cook for 2 minutes less than the packet instructions, as the pasta will continue to cook off the heat. The sauce should be reduced and the consistency of half-sauce, half-soup…so a bit of a wet sloppy pasta sauce (but in a delicious way). Adjust the consistency as needed with additional water, stock, or bean liquid, keeping in mind that any liquid will tighten up as it cools due to starch from the beans and pasta.

For the flavoured oil, add 4 tablespoons of extra virgin olive oil to a pan with the garlic, rosemary and chilli flakes, while the oil is still cold, so that the garlic cooks evenly and not too quickly.
Gently cook for 3–4 minutes until fragrant and the garlic is lightly golden, then turn off the heat and squeeze in the lemon juice.

Remove the pasta from heat and add most of the grated Parmesan, leaving some to serve and stir rapidly to incorporate and become creamy. Ladle a few spoonfuls into bowls, then drizzle each serving with the flavoured olive oil and the reserved Parmesan.

# My Perfect Bean and Tuna Lunch

This is a truly anytime, all day meal – it's perfect for those occasions when you just want something small and simple to share between two. People who know me would say this is a very me plate of food!

**Serves 2**

4 tablespoons extra virgin olive oil
1 banana shallot or onion, finely chopped
1 celery stick, finely diced
1 garlic clove, grated
pinch of chilli (hot pepper) flakes (optional)
1 teaspoon spices of choice, such as fennel seeds or turmeric
1 x 400 g (14 oz) tin of chickpeas, (garbanzo beans) or cannellini beans, or 400 g (14 oz) Beans for the Week (page 15)
juice of ½ lemon, plus extra wedges to serve
2 eggs (or however many you want)
150 g (5½ oz) kale or cavolo nero (lacinato kale), stalks removed and leaves torn
1 x 150 g (5½ oz) tin of tuna in olive oil
small handful of dill, finely chopped
sea salt and freshly ground black pepper

**For the breadcrumbs**
2 tablespoons olive oil
50 g (1¾ oz/scant ⅔ cup) fresh breadcrumbs
1 heaped tablespoon capers, drained
1 garlic clove, grated
zest of ½ lemon

Heat 3 tablespoons of the oil in a small saucepan over a medium heat and fry the shallot or onion and the celery with a pinch of salt until soft but not coloured, about 5 minutes. Stir in the garlic and chilli flakes and spices, if using, then cook for a further 2 minutes until fragrant. Pour in the beans with half their juices (or 100 ml/3½ fl oz/scant ½ cup stock or water) and stir. Gently bubble and heat through for 3–5 minutes, then remove from the heat and add the lemon juice. Taste and adjust the seasoning as needed.

Next, make the breadcrumbs. Heat the oil in a small frying pan (skillet) over a medium-high heat and stir in the breadcrumbs and capers so they are coated in the oil. Fry for 4–6 minutes until crisp, then add the garlic for a final minute. Remove from the heat, add the lemon zest and set aside.

Boil the eggs in a large saucepan of boiling water for 7 minutes, then lift the eggs out and refresh under cold water. Add the greens to the same pan and boil for 2 minutes, then drain and transfer back into the empty pan. Drizzle with the remaining oil and season with a pinch of salt and pepper.

Serve the warm beans with a small pile of the greens, the boiled eggs, a few chunks of tuna, the breadcrumbs, chopped dill and a wedge of lemon.

# Grated Tomatoes and White Beans

This is basically the topping for the classic Spanish dish pan con tomate (bread with tomatoes), but mixed with cannellini beans. I grew up on versions of this traditional recipe, and it's the best way both to champion a good tomato or to use up a tomato that's a little sad and past its best for a salad.

This beany version is especially perfect with fish and aioli (page 158), which is how I eat it in Mallorca, but I'm equally as happy with it on its own with crusty bread and anchovies.

**Serves 2**

2–3 beef tomatoes or 4–6 vine tomatoes (ideally the best that summer can give you!)
2 tablespoons best-quality extra virgin olive oil
1 teaspoon red wine vinegar or lemon juice
1 x 400 g (14 oz) tin of cannellini beans, drained, or or 400 g (14 oz) Beans for the Week (page 15)
sea salt and freshly ground black pepper

**To serve**
toasted sourdough
anchovy fillets

Coarsely grate the tomatoes into a bowl, then season generously with salt. Give it a mix, then pour into a fine sieve set over a bowl to catch any juices. Leave to sit for 5 minutes.

Pour the collected juices into a glass (I drink this with some ice… it's so good!), then add the grated tomatoes back into the bowl along with the oil, vinegar or lemon juice, and some black pepper.

Stir the drained beans into the tomatoes, then serve with chunks of toasted sourdough bread and anchovies to drape over.

# Onion Butter Beans with Crispy Garlic and Pickled Chillies

This is great as a dip or a side. It's essentially a form of hummus but with loads of extra-good crispy and pickled bits.

**Serves 2 as a side**

2 tablespoons extra virgin olive oil
1 onion, finely chopped
1 garlic clove, grated or finely
  chopped
pinch of chilli (hot pepper) flakes,
  plus extra to serve (optional)
1 x 400 g (14 oz) tin of butter
  (lima) beans, chickpeas
  (garbanzo beans) or cannellini
  beans, or 400 g (14 oz) Beans
  for the Week (page 15)
juice of ½ lemon
sea salt and freshly ground
  black pepper
flatbreads or other fresh bread,
  to serve
flaky sea salt, to serve

**For the garlic chilli butter**
25 g (1 oz) butter (or another
  tablespoon extra virgin olive oil)
1 tablespoon extra virgin olive oil
3 garlic cloves, finely sliced
few heaped tablespoons pickled
  jalapeños or other pickled
  chillies, finely chopped
1 teaspoon za'atar (optional)
small handful of fresh herbs, such
  as parsley or coriander (cilantro),
  leaves finely chopped

Heat the oil in a saucepan or casserole dish (Dutch oven) over a medium heat. Add the onion and a pinch of salt and gently fry for 10–12 minutes, adding more oil if you need to, until really soft and slightly caramelised. The more time and love you give the onion at this stage, the better this is going to taste. Add the garlic and chili flakes, if using, and cook for a further 2–3 minutes until fragrant.

Drain the beans, reserving 2 tablespoons of the liquid from the tin, then add both to a food processor with the onion, lemon juice and a generous pinch of salt. Blend until smooth. At this point you can scrape the bean purée into a pan and gently warm it up, but I don't mind it being just warmed from the onions, or even cold.

In the same saucepan you cooked the onions, make the garlic chilli butter: heat the butter and oil over a medium heat until foaming, then add the garlic. Swirl the pan and let the garlic crisp up for 2 minutes before adding the pickled chillies and za'atar, if using, along with a few grinds of black pepper. Remove from the heat, then stir in the herbs.

Dollop the bean purée onto a plate or platter and spoon over the garlic and herb butter.

Sprinkle with a little flaky sea salt, then serve with the flatbreads or bread.

# Ricotta, Charred Corn and Curried Onions

Eating corn on the cob straight from the cob, with your hands dripping with butter, is surely the best and most simple thing there is. I can't argue with the simplicity of it, but this recipe takes little effort and tastes great. I realise it has a lot of butter...but corn just tastes better with it. Serve with a stack of bread, stir a tin of beans into the corn for a more hearty meal, or simply serve as a side.

**Serves 2, or 4 as a side**

1 x 250 g (9 oz) tub of ricotta
2 corn on the cob or 250 g (9 oz) tinned sweetcorn
3 tablespoons vegetable or olive oil
2 onions, finely sliced
60 g (2 oz) butter
2 garlic cloves, grated
1 teaspoon curry powder
small handful of chives, finely chopped
zest and juice of 1 lime
sea salt
crusty bread, to serve

Empty the ricotta into a bowl and mix well until smooth.

Slice the corn off the cob by laying the corn down on a chopping board and slicing one side off. This will allow you to rest the flat side down and slice the rest off easily.

Heat a large, dry frying pan (skillet) over a high heat and, once hot, add the corn. Char the corn for 4–6 minutes, stirring only once or twice until some parts are a little blackened and the corn is cooked. If using tinned corn, drain the corn and leave it to dry a little in a sieve. If the corn is still particularly damp from the tin, transfer it to a dish towel and give it a rub, then char in the pan as above (you won't need to cook it for quite so long as the corn is already cooked). Tip the charred corn onto a plate and set aside.

Heat the oil in same pan over a medium heat. Add the onions with a pinch of salt and gently fry for 20–25 minutes, adding a little more oil if needed, until really soft and slightly caramelised. Put some time into cooking the onions, as this is an essential part of the dish.

Add the butter to the onions, along with the garlic and curry powder, and allow to bubble for a minute, stirring to toast the curry powder. Tip the corn back into the pan and give it a stir, followed by three-quarters of the chives and the lime zest and juice.

Dollop the ricotta onto a plate or platter, then pile on the corn and onions and finish with the remaining chives. Serve hot with some crusty bread.

# Scraps Pasta

This dish has a spaghetti aglio, olio e pepperoncino vibe, but using fresh courgette (zuchinni) ribbons and broken sheets of lasagne instead of the classic long pasta. You can use any pasta you like here, but I always seem to have some lingering lasagne sheets at the back of the cupboard and I like their fresh silkiness coupled with the courgette.

**Serves 2**

1 large or 2 medium courgettes (zucchini)
4 tablespoons olive oil
2 banana shallots or 1 onion, thinly sliced
2 tablespoons capers, drained
2 large garlic cloves, thinly sliced
½ red chilli, finely chopped or 1 teaspoon chilli (hot pepper) flakes
180–200 g (6¼–7 oz) lasagne sheets, roughly broken up
20–30 g (¾–1 oz) Parmesan, grated
½ bunch of basil or parsley, leaves picked and roughly chopped
sea salt and freshly ground black pepper

Peel the courgette into ribbons using a vegetable peeler until you're left with a long stump. Finely chop the middle bit into 5 mm (¼ inch) chunks and set aside.

Heat the oil in a frying pan (skillet) over a medium-low heat and fry the shallots and capers for 8–10 minutes, or until the shallots are golden at the edges and the capers have collapsed. Add the courgette chunks (not the ribbons), garlic, chilli and a pinch of salt a cook for a further 2–3 minutes until the garlic is soft but not catching and the courgette is just cooked. Remove from the heat.

Bring a saucepan of salted water to the boil and cook the lasagne sheets according to the packet instructions. Add the courgette ribbons for the last minute until just cooked. Using tongs, lift the pasta and courgettes out of the water and add them directly to the pan of shallots, along with a few splashes of the pasta water. Add half the Parmesan and most of the basil leaves and stir to combine, then divide between bowls and top with the rest of the Parmesan, the remaining basil and a few grinds of black pepper.

# Tonnato Salad

I love tuna (specifically tinned tuna) and I regularly crave some sort of tuna salad, but sometimes I just want more – more of a meal, more tuna flavour, more crunchiness. So, here is my non-traditional take on a tonnato (the Italian dish of thinly sliced pork with a tuna sauce). In this version, the tonnato sauce is tossed with warm boiled potatoes and crunchy vegetables.

Feel free to add any type of salad and crunchy vegetables that are in your refrigetator, such as broccoli, peas or broad (fava) beans.

**Serves 2, or 4 as a side**

500 g (1 lb 2 oz) new or Charlotte potatoes, large ones halved
100 g (3½ oz) fine green beans, trimmed
handful of soft herbs, finely chopped – I like dill and parsley for this
extra virgin olive oil, for drizzling
1 cucumber, peeled and chopped
1 Little Gem or romaine lettuce
1 red onion, thinly sliced

**For the tonnato sauce**

1 x 145 g (5 oz) tin of tuna in olive oil, drained
2 tablespoons plain yoghurt or mayonnaise
1 tablespoons capers, drained
zest and juice of 1 lemon
2 tablespoons good-quality extra virgin olive oil
sea salt and freshly ground black pepper

Start by making the tonnato sauce. Combine all the ingredients in a food processor with some salt and pepper and a splash of water and blend until smooth. It should have the consistency of a thick dressing – if not, add more water as needed.

Add the potatoes to a saucepan of lightly salted cold water, then bring to the boil and cook for about 10 minutes until soft. After 6 minutes, add the green beans and cook with the potatoes for the remaining 4 minutes.

Drain the potatoes and green beans, then drain them under cold water to cool slightly.

Add the herbs, torn lettuce and red onion to the potatoes with a good drizzle of extra virgin olive oil and some salt and pepper. Toss together.

Spoon the sauce onto a platter, pile on the cucumber and finish with the potatoes.

# Brown Butter, Oat and Anything Cookies

These cookies take 25 minutes to make from start to finish and you'll most definitely have everything at home right now, so they're great for when you just really want something sweet ASAP. You can add anything you want for flavour. I've included ground ginger here, but ground cardamom, cinnamon, lemon or zest, crushed fennel seeds, grated fresh root ginger or just vanilla extract would be great too. They work without an egg, too, so if you haven't got one, don't stress, they'll just be more like crisp biscuits than chewy cookies.

**Makes 12**

150 g (5½ oz/1½ cups) rolled
    oats
90 g (6¾ oz/¾ cup) plain
    (all-purpose) flour
½ teaspoon baking powder
pinch of flaky sea salt
1 teaspoon ground ginger
    (optional)
110 g (4 oz) unsalted butter
80 g (2¾ oz/⅓ cup) caster
    (superfine) sugar
2 tablespoons honey (or golden
    syrup/light corn syrup or
    maple syrup)
1 egg, beaten
50–75 g (1¾–2½ oz)
    chocolate, dried fruit or nuts
    (or a mixture)

Preheat the oven to 180°C fan (400°F) and line two baking sheets with baking parchment.

Combine the oats, flour, baking powder, salt and ground ginger, if using, in a large bowl.

Gently melt the butter in a small saucepan for 4–5 minutes until the butter starts to foam, turn a very light golden brown and smell sweet and nutty like caramel. Add the sugar and honey and remove from the heat, then set aside to cool for 5 minutes.

Pour the butter mixture into the flour and oats, along with the egg and chocolate, dried fruit and/or nuts. Stir until it forms a stiff mixture and everything is evenly combined.

Scoop 12 heaped tablespoons of the mixture onto the prepared baking sheets with at least 5 cm (2 inches) between each one as they will spread when cooking. Bake for 15 minutes until very lightly golden brown.

Remove from the oven and allow to cool for 15 minutes.

# POTATOES

# ONIONS

# MY PERFECT POTATO

Potato Cakes (page 41)

My Perfect Potato (page 40), roasted in olive oil until crispy

Mum's Ham Cakes with Parsley Sauce (page 46)

My Perfect Potato (page 40)

Potato Gnocchi (page 41)

Cheat's Spanish Tortilla (page 42)

# MY PERFECT POTATO

This page is supposed to be a potato recipe, but it just didn't make sense to write one to suit all. There are 4,000 different potato varieties and each one tastes and acts differently. So how can I show you how to best use yours? I can't cover them all!

Instead, I'm here to share my ode to the perfect boiled potato. Floury or new potatoes. Cooked in the most basic way, to make the best of the sides. Over the next few pages I've put together simple ways to use up that perfect boiled potato – beige in all its glory. Crisp them up, mash them into potato cakes or knead them into gnocchi (next page), slice them into tortilla (page 42), or just toss with aioli (page 158), capers and herbs for a potato salad.

Potatoes are one of the UK's most wasted items, and I can't imagine why! They last, they are versatile and, of course, delicious. There are unlimited ways to cook a potato and I love them all. The potato is the ultimate symbol of simplicity and each person has their favourite. 'If you could only eat a potato in one way, how would you eat it?' I truly think mine would be the perfect boiled potato. Tossed in butter, parsley (plus an occasional dollop of mustard) and plenty of flaky salt and pepper, there are few things more comforting. It suits summer and winter, fish, meat or veg. It's the side to suit and please all.

My mum boils small floury potatoes with their skins still on, then allows them to steam in the colander for a few minutes before peeling off the boiling hot skin with her hands. I try to peel a few and can barely hold one for a second. She peels with ease, leaving a pile of perfectly smooth mismatched pale potatoes waiting to be tossed in cubes of butter or drizzled in extra virgin olive oil. I can't decide which is better, so it's up to you.

So look again at your basket of sprouting potatoes, give them a scrub, chop into equal large pieces and place them in a large pot of cold water. Bring to the boil and cook for 12–18 minutes until soft right through. Drain, then allow to steam before carefully peeling off the skin and eating them as is, or following any of my ideas in the next few pages.

# Potato Gnocchi

A great thing about my job is that sometimes I have to cook things I would never think of making at home. In my mind (and I think a lot of people think the same), potato gnocchi seems a hard thing to master and an impressive thing to make from scratch. But it's not! It's two ingredients and if you've got leftover potatoes then it's even easier.

Ideally make the mash as fine as you can, as this will result in a better gnocchi. I push the potato through a sieve with a back of a spoon as I don't own a ricer. These are delicious simply crisped up in a pan with butter and sage, but I also love them served with the Green Sauce from page 60.

**Serves 3–4**

500 g (1 lb 2 oz) Maris Piper or any floury potatoes (or about 550 g/1 lb 3 oz leftover boiled potatoes, see opposite)
50 g (1¾ oz/scant ½ cup) 00 flour or plain (all-purpose) flour, plus extra for dusting
sea salt and freshly ground black pepper

If you're cooking the potatoes from scratch, try to use potatoes that are of similar size as you want them to cook at the same time. Add the potatoes whole to a pan and cover with cold water. Add a large pinch of salt, then bring to the boil and cook for 20–25 minutes until soft.

Drain in a colander to steam and cook for at least 15 minutes, then peel off the skins. Mash the potatoes until smooth as can be, then sprinkle over the flour, along with a another pinch of salt and pepper. Mix the flour into the potatoes (I like to use my hands here) until it just comes together. You may need a little extra flour depending on your potatoes, but careful not to add too much as this can make them chewy. Tip out onto a clean surface with a sprinkling of flour, then knead for a minute. Divide into 4 pieces, then roll each one into a long sausage about 2 cm (¾ inch) thick. Slice into 2 cm (¾ inch) gnocchi, then squeeze a little with your fingers.

Cook the gnocchi in a pan of boiling salted water for 2–3 minutes or until they float to the top. Scoop them out of the pan into your sauce of choice. Melted butter, lots of black pepper and Parmesan is a classic, as is a tomato sauce, or the green sauce from page 62 would be great.

### To make Potato Cakes
Use any leftover gnocchi dough, or the whole recipe quantity, to make potato cakes – simply roll out the dough into a circular shape, cut into triangles and toast in a pan over a medium heat until crispy.

# Cheat's Spanish Tortilla

I've been eating tortillas all my life – proper ones, too. The ones that are 10 cm (4 inches) high and with that distinct, onion-y, potato-y taste that I love so much. I love making them and I find immense satisfaction in getting that perfect, light golden dome. But making traditional tortillas is not the easiest. You need a special pan, a LOT of olive oil, and quite a bit of time. So here is my cheat's version, which I make when I'm craving the flavours but don't want the fuss.

Be creative with the potatoes here – you can use any leftovers you have lying around, from new potatoes to roast potatoes, or even chips (French fries). If you want to scale up the recipe, just increase the number of eggs to match how many people you're serving.

**Serves 4**

4 glugs of good-quality extra
 virgin olive oil
2 small onions or 4 banana
 shallots, halved and thinly sliced
100 g (3½ oz) leftover cooked
 potatoes (page 40), sliced
 into 1 cm (½ inch) rounds
 or small chunks
2–4 medium eggs (depending on
 how hungry you are)
sea salt and freshly ground
 black pepper

**To serve (optional)**
bread
anchovy fillets
slices of ham
pickled green chillies, chopped
parsley leaves or chives, chopped

Heat the oil in a medium frying pan (skillet) over a medium heat. About 20 cm (8 inches) diameter is ideal as you want everything to be quite snug. It might seem like a lot of oil, but this is key to the flavour of the dish, and any excess is used to fry the eggs at the end.

Add the onions to the pan along with a good pinch of salt and cook for 10–15 minutes until very soft, golden and caramelised, stirring often so they don't catch.

Use a fork to lift the onions out of the pan and set aside on a plate, leaving the oil in the pan. Add the potato slices or chunks and cook for about 5 minutes, flipping them regularly until they are very lightly browned on all sides.

Turn up the heat a little and make a space in the pan to crack an egg into. Then make another gap, pushing the potatoes to one side and cracking the egg into the oily gap. Lay the onions on top of the potatoes and eggs, then season the yolks with salt and pepper and cook for 3–4 minutes, depending on how you like your eggs.

Finish with your chosen toppings, then either eat out of the pan like me or serve at the table with mounds of bread and any extras – I love anchovies or ham, pickled green chillies and parsley leaves or chives.

# Baked Leek and Mustard Mashed Potato

A friend of mine, the photographer Issy Croker, makes this at Christmas time, and it's so impressive when she puts the hot, steaming, crunchy-topped mash on the table. It's a crowd pleaser! If you don't have leeks, I'd recommend using a bunch of spring onions (scallions) instead – they'll also cook quicker, so it's a handy swap if you don't have much time. Side note: this is also very delicious made with mash that you can find in the ready meals section of the supermarket. Just add this to the pan with the leeks and milk and you're ready to go! You can use any leftover boiled potatoes you have (page 40) and adjust as necessary.

## Serves 4

1 kg (2 lb 4 oz) floury potatoes, such as Maris Pipers or King Edwards, peeled and chopped into 4 cm (1½ inch) chunks
50 g (1¾ oz) butter
2 garlic cloves, finely chopped
4 leeks, trimmed, washed and sliced into 1 cm (½ inch) rounds
5 sprigs of thyme, leaves picked
140 ml (4¾ fl oz/scant ⅔ cup) milk
150 g (5½ oz) Cheddar, Parmesan or Gruyère, grated
2 tablespoons Dijon mustard
sea salt and freshly ground black pepper

Boil the potatoes in a large saucepan of boiling water for 20 minutes until soft, then drain and leave to steam in the colander while you cook the leeks.

Place the empty pan back over a medium heat and melt the butter, then add the garlic and fry for 1 minute until fragrant. Add the leeks, thyme leaves and a pinch of salt. Stir, then cover with a lid and cook for 20–25 minutes until really soft, adding a splash of water if the leeks start to caramelise. Add the milk and allow to warm through, then remove from the heat.

Mash the potatoes until smooth. (For really smooth mash, push the potatoes through a sieve with a wooden spoon.) Add the potatoes to the milk and leek mixture, along with half the cheese, the mustard, a pinch of salt and plenty of black pepper. Stir until smooth. At this point, you can enjoy it as it is or take it one step further, which I really recommend.

Heat the oven to 200°C fan (425°F). Spoon the mash into a 20 x 30 cm (8 x 12 inches) deep baking dish (don't use anything too big, as you're looking for a crunchy top and lots of light, fluffy mash underneath). Level it out, then sprinkle over the remaining cheese.

Bake in the oven for 15–20 minutes until crisp and golden. I recommend you leave this to cool slightly for 10 minutes before serving as the inside will be very hot! Any leftovers can be used to make potato cakes (page 41).

# Mum's Ham Cakes with Parsley Sauce

This might be my desert island dish… My family beg my mum to make this every Christmas, or any time there is leftover ham or potatoes of any type. There is nothing fancy about them, but that's what makes them home cooking (and leftovers cooking) at its best. The ham can also be replaced with 250 g (9 oz) skinless fish fillets such as salmon, trout, cod or haddock, or chopped prawns (or a mixture), or even just left out to make a vegetarian version.

**Makes 10**

750 g (1 lb 10 oz) floury potatoes, such as Maris Pipers or King Edwards, peeled and cut into 2 cm ¾ inch) chunks (or 650 g/1 lb 7 oz leftover boiled potatoes, page 40)
200 g (7 oz) ham hock or sliced ham, chopped
25 g (1 oz) parsley leaves, chopped
bunch of spring onions (scallions), chopped
2 tablespoons capers, drained, plus extra to serve
1 tablespoon Dijon mustard
1 egg, beaten
1 x quantity of Parsley Sauce (page 139)
sea salt and freshly ground black pepper

If cooking the potatoes from scratch, put them into a saucepan with enough water to cover and ½ teaspoon salt. Bring to the boil and cook for 12–15 minutes until soft, then drain and set aside to steam dry and cool in the colander for at least 5 minutes. The potatoes need to be very dry for this recipe, so let them steam for as long as you can.

Once cooled and dried, crush the potatoes in a large bowl. Don't mash them completely – you want it to be a very lumpy mash. Mix in the ham, parsley, spring onions, capers, mustard, egg and 300 g (10½ oz) of the parsley sauce along with a generous pinch of salt and pepper. Stir it all together carefully, making sure it's evenly combined but not totally mashed together.

Form the mixture into tennis-ball sized patties (about 120 g/4¼ oz each) and place onto a baking sheet or large plate. Refrigerate to set for a minimum of 1 hour.

You can pat the ham cakes down and fry them like this if you don't have the time or the ingredients to coat them, but I like to coat them with breadcrumbs for extra crunch.

Put the flour into a bowl, seasoning with a pinch of salt and pepper. Put the breadcrumbs into another bowl and put the beaten eggs into a third bowl. Set up an empty baking tray (pan) at the end, ready to put the ham cakes onto once breaded.

Mould the ham cakes into the shape you want – I like to pat mine into neat 2 cm (¾ inch) thick patties. Dip the patties into the flour, making sure it covers every side, then into the beaten eggs, again making sure the egg coats all the surfaces, then finally into the breadcrumbs.

**For coating and frying**

100 g (3½ oz/generous ¾ cup)
  plain (all-purpose) flour
200 g (7 oz/2½ cups) fresh,
  dried or panko breadcrumbs
2 eggs, beaten
3–4 tablespoons neutral oil
25 g (1 oz) salted butter

You can freeze or refrigerate some of the ham cakes at this stage, then just fry however many you want to eat.

Heat the oil and butter in a large frying pan (skillet) over a medium-high heat, then add a few ham cakes at a time, sealing off the edges first by rolling them in the butter and oil until lightly golden. Take care as they will be quite fragile. Turn over and fry for 3–4 minutes on each side until completely golden all over.

Spoon a generous amount of parsley sauce onto a plate, followed by a crispy ham cake and a few extra capers.

# Jacket Potatoes and Jacket Onions

Don't laugh at me – yes, I'm writing a recipe for jacket potatoes. This is mostly to remind you that they are great, and that if you're having friends over, you should make jacket potatoes! Everyone loves them, they are so cheap and the opportunities for how to serve them (and for what to do with any leftovers) are endless. The trick is to roast onions at the same time – you'll see why. Thank me later.

I like to serve this with a big green salad, but you can also serve the onions with toasted sourdough and a cheese of your choice.

**Serves 4**

4 large baking potatoes
4 large onions, unpeeled
2 tablespoons olive oil
10 grinds of freshly ground black
   pepper, plus extra to serve
flaky sea salt

**To serve**
salted butter
Cheddar
chopped chives

Preheat the oven to 200°C fan (425°F)

Pierce the whole, unpeeled potatoes and onions all over with a knife.

If you have a microwave, this is where it comes in handy. (I love microwaves…!) Place the potatoes and onions in the microwave (you might have to do the onions and potatoes separately if they don't all fit) and cook on high for 10 minutes until semi-soft. (If you don't have a microwave, just skip this step and roast them in the oven for longer.)

Remove the potatoes and onions from the microwave and place them in a roasting tin with the olive oil, pepper and plenty of salt. Jiggle the tray so that the oil completely coats the vegetables. Roast in the oven for 30 minutes (or 1 hour if not using a microwave first) until the skins of the potatoes are crisp and golden and the insides of both vegetables are really soft when pierced with a knife.

Remove the tin from the oven and transfer the potatoes and onions to a platter (or sometimes I just serve in the tin!). Slice a cross shape in the top of the vegetables, then press the sides to open them up.

Add a knob of butter to each, along with a pinch of flaky sea salt and a good grind of black pepper, then top with a chunk of cheese and a small mound of freshly chopped chives. Serve with extra cheese and butter for topping up.

# Lemon Roast Potatoes with Cucumber and Honey Yoghurt

These potatoes are cooked Greek style, which means adding liquid to the roasting tray. This steams the potatoes, then as they soak up the lemony liquid they start to crisp up, resulting in the most flavourful, crispy potatoes. You can serve these with anything – obviously, I'm going to say with a roast chicken (page 88) – but I'd equally have them with on their own or with a big green salad in the summer.

**Serves 4**

1.2 kg (2 lb 11 oz) floury potatoes, such as Maris Pipers or King Edwards, peeled and cut into 3 cm (1¼ inch) thick wedges
2 lemons, 1 juiced and 1 sliced into 1 cm (½ inch) half-moons
200 ml (7 fl oz/scant 1 cup) chicken or vegetable stock
100 ml (3½ fl oz/scant ½ cup) extra virgin olive oil
5 garlic cloves, peeled and left whole
few sprigs of fresh oregano or 1 tablespoon dried oregano
generous pinch of salt

**For the cucumber and honey yoghurt**
200 g (7 oz) Greek yoghurt
½ cucumber, coursely grated
3 tablespoons extra virgin olive oil
1 tablespoon honey
pinch of flaky sea salt
small handful of fresh mint, leaves picked and larger leaves chopped

Preheat the oven to 200°C fan (425°F).

Place the potatoes in a large, high-sided roasting tin (pan) with the lemon slices and lemon juice, stock, olive oil, garlic cloves, oregano and salt. Toss everything together, then spread the potatoes out in a single layer – this is important so that they all cook and crisp up evenly. Roast in the oven for 20 minutes. After this time, turn the potatoes over, then place back in the oven for a further 25–30 minutes until the liquid has been absorbed by the potatoes and you're left with a lemony oil at the bottom of the tray. Half the potatoes should be crispy and half still soft.

In a small bowl, stir together all the ingredients for the cucumber and honey yoghurt.

Pile the potatoes on to a platter and serve with a dollop of the yoghurt.

# Very Oniony Pasta with Parmesan and Black Pepper

I love French onion soup … a lot. Actually, I just love onions in general. This dish is a marriage of French onion soup, cacio e pepe and a storecupboard pasta recipe. It comes together very easily with minimal ingredients. I've served it plain here, but it's also great with parsley and the crispy breadcrumbs from page 116.

**Serves 2**

3 tablespoons olive oil
3 onions, halved and very thinly
  sliced
120 g (4¼ oz) spaghetti (or any
  pasta you have)
2 cloves garlic, finely chopped
½ red chilli, deseeded and finely
  chopped (or a pinch of chilli/hot
  pepper flakes; optional)
4–5 anchovy fillets (optional)
100 ml (3½ fl oz/scant
  ½ cup) water
zest and juice of ½ lemon
40 g (1½ oz) Parmesan, grated
small handful of parsley, very
  finely chopped (optional)
sea salt and freshly ground
  black pepper

Heat the oil in a large saucepan or casserole dish (Dutch oven) over a medium-low heat. Add the onions and a pinch of salt and gently fry for 15 minutes until very soft and translucent, stirring often and adding a little more oil if you need to. Turn up the heat a little and fry for a further 5–8 minutes until very soft and slightly caramelised. Put some time into cooking the onions here as they are such an essential part of this dish – the more love you give the onions, the better this is going to taste. If they start to catch and caramelise before they are soft, simply add as splash of water and continue.

Alternatively, if you have a microwave, use it to get things started (I do!). Put the chopped onions into a microwaveable container or bowl with the oil and salt and cover with cling film (plastic wrap) or a loose-fitting lid, then microwave on high for 10 minutes, stirring halfway until translucent and really soft. After this time, transfer to a pan and finish cooking to caramelise the onions.

Cook the pasta in a large saucepan of salted boiling water according to the packet instructions. Reserve a large mugful of the pasta water before draining – this is very important!

Meanwhile, add the garlic to the onions, along with the chilli and anchovies, if using. Fry for 2 minutes before adding a generous splash of pasta water. The onions and garlic should soak up the water and become soft, sort of like an onion ragu. Continue to gently bubble on medium-low for 5 minutes. Add the lemon zest and juice and about 15 grinds of freshly ground black pepper, then turn the heat down to the lowest it will go. Taste and check for seasoning.

Add the drained pasta and Parmesan, along with half a mugful of pasta water and parsley, if using. Mix until the sauce thickens a little but is loose enough to coat every strand of spaghetti. Sometimes I need a full mug of the pasta water to get the right consistency, so keep mixing and tossing until you're happy. Serve immediately.

# Crispy Salmon and Double Onion

This recipe might be my most cooked in the book. I'm a sucker for anything that involves chilli oil and rice! Something that I do often is just cook the onions, chilli, garlic and ginger, then remove from the pan and add some whisked eggs to make a simple omelette. Then serve that with the onions, fresh spring onions (scallions) and rice. My go-to 10-minute dinner.

**Serves 2 or 4 with sides**

5 tablespoons olive oil
2 onions or 4 banana shallots, thinly sliced
½ red chilli, deseeded and finely sliced
3 cm (1¼ inch) piece of fresh root ginger, peeled and grated
3 garlic cloves, grated
500 g (1 lb 2 oz) salmon fillet (in one piece or 4 smaller fillets)
bunch of spring onions (scallions)
sea salt

**To serve**
½ cucumber, finely diced
1 x quantity Garlic, Ginger and Chilli Green Oil (page 68)
jasmine rice

Preheat the oven to 200°C fan (425°F).

Heat 3 tablespoons of the oil in an ovenproof frying pan (skillet) over a medium heat and, once hot, add the onions and a pinch of salt and fry for 8–10 minutes until just starting to soften. They will cook further in the oven, so don't worry about cooking them fully. Add the chilli, ginger, garlic and cook for a further 2 minutes, then scoop out of the pan and set aside on a plate.

Season the salmon with salt on all sides.

Add the remaining oil to the pan and turn the heat up to high. Place the salmon skin-side down in the frying pan and leave to fry for 5–8 minutes until the salmon skin is crisp. Add the spring onions, placing them around the salmon, then transfer the pan to the oven and cook for 15 minutes until the salmon is cooked through (this will depend on how thick the piece of fish is).

Remove the salmon and onions from the oven and carefully scoop everything onto a platter.

Combine the cucumber with the green oil in a small bowl.

Serve with a bowl of steaming jasmine rice and the cucumber and green oil.

# VEGETABLES AND HERBS

Green Sauce (page 60) with Roast Chicken (pages 88–89) and Aioli (page 158)

Green Sauce (page 60) stirred into pasta

Lettuce with Green Goddess dressing (page 62) and Breadcrumbs (page 114)

Green Sauce (page 60) on toast

Green Soup (page 64)

All Greens Gallette (page 63)

# GREEN SAUCE

This is may be one of my favourite things to eat and make. It's ever-changing, and never the same twice, but I've tried to sum up what I do here. It is the start to so many amazing things to eat and I always have a jar in the refrigerator. My favourite way to eat it is with the roast chicken from pages 88-89 and the aioli from page 158. Or stirred through pasta!

**Makes 1 x large jar**

1 garlic clove, peeled
150 g (5½ oz) spinach, cavolo
   nero (lacinato kale), chard or
   kale (stalks removed and leaves
   shredded if necessary)
handful (15 g) of parsley
handful (20 g) of basil leaves
30 g (1 oz) Parmesan, grated
6–8 tablespoons good-quality
   extra virgin olive oil, plus extra
zest and juice of 1 lemon
sea salt and freshly ground
   black pepper

**To serve**
1 x 200 g (7 oz) tub of ricotta
toasted sourdough
anchovy fillets (optional)

Bring a large saucepan of salted water to the boil and add the garlic. Boil for 2 minutes, then add the spinach (or other greens), parsley and basil to the boiling water and blanch for 30 seconds until wilted and bright green. Drain and refresh under cold water for a minute or so until cooled.

Using your hands, squeeze as much water out of the greens and herbs as you can, then transfer to a food processor with the garlic, Parmesan, olive oil, lemon zest and juice and a good pinch of salt and a few a grinds of black pepper. Blend until completely smooth, adding a little more oil until you're happy with the texture. For spreading on toast, I like it a little thicker, but for pasta I prefer it a little silkier and smoother. It's important to taste it here – each lemon gives a different amount of juice and each type of herb and vegetable can be a little more bitter or sweet, so if it needs more salt or even more Parmesan, go for it!

Spread the ricotta over the toast and top with the green sauce, an extra drizzle of olive oil and the anchovies, if using.

If you don't use it all, transfer it to a container and cover it with oil to preserve it, then store in the refrigerator for up to 5 days.

---

**Serves 2, or 4 as a side**

2 heaped tablespoons Green
   Sauce (see above)
1 tablespoon natural yoghurt
1 tablespoon tahini (optional)
splash of water

**To serve**
4 or 5 handfuls of salad leaves
Crispy Breadcrumbs (page 114)

## Green Goddess Dressing

Add the green sauce, yoghurt, tahini and water to a large bowl and stir until everything is incorporated and it is the consistency you want.

Add the salad mix, then give everything a toss. Serve immediately topped with breadcrumbs.

# All Greens Galette

Same green sauce, but this time used in a versatile tart. You can take this any way you like, depending on what's in season. Here, I've used asparagus, but courgettes (zucchini), mushrooms or thinly sliced potatoes would also be great.

**Serves 4–6**

2 medium eggs or 1 large
100 g (3½ oz) ricotta, crème fraiche, mascarpone or cream cheese, plus extra to serve
1 x quantity Green Sauce (see page 60)
bunch of asparagus, ends trimmed
2 tablespoons olive oil
500 g (1 lb 2 oz) block puff pastry (or homemade pastry, see below)
fennel seeds or sesame seeds, for sprinkling
sea salt and freshly ground black pepper

Preheat the oven to 200°C fan (425°F).

Beat the eggs in a large bowl, then remove and reserve a tablespoon of the beaten egg in a glass for later. Tip the ricotta and green sauce into the beaten eggs and whisk together until evenly combined.

In a bowl, toss the asparagus (or your chosen veg) with the oil and a pinch of salt and pepper.

Roll out the pastry into a 30 cm (12 inch) round, about 1 cm (½ inch) thick (it's OK if it's a little misshapen), then lay the pastry on a lined baking sheet.

Spoon the cheese and green sauce mixture into the middle of the pastry, leaving a 4 cm (1½ inch) border. Add the dressed asparagus, then fold the excess pastry over the edges. Brush the pastry with the reserved egg and sprinkle with the fennel or sesame seeds and a pinch of salt, then bake in the oven for 35 minutes until golden.

**To make your own pastry (It's easy – don't be scared!)**

360 g (12½ oz/scant 3 cups) plain (all-purpose) flour
1 teaspoon fine salt
285 g (10 oz) cold unsalted butter, cut into small cubes
60ml (2 fl oz/¼ cup) ice-cold water
1 tablespoon apple cider vinegar or white wine vinegar

Combine the flour and salt in a large bowl. Add the butter, then use your fingertips to rub the butter into the flour until you have a chunky breadcrumb texture. Be careful not to overwork the mixture – you still want a few chunks of butter left (this will make it puff and rise).

Mix the water with the vinegar in a glass or jug (pitcher), then slowly pour the water into the flour and butter, lightly mixing it as you go until you have a very rough dough. Once you rest the dough, you'll be surprised by how much it hydrates, so don't worry if it looks dry.

Press the dough into one compact mass, then wrap in cling film (plastic wrap) and refrigerate for a minimum of 2 hours. The longer you leave it, the better it will be, so this can be made up to 4 days before baking.

When you're ready to bake, remove the pastry from the refrigerator 10 minutes before rolling it out.

# Green Soup

This is when having a jar of green sauce in the refrigerator really comes in handy. A dollop of this in a bowl, with hot stock poured over and some simple veg and pasta is the easiest meal you can pull together. A lot of the time I just add frozen peas! I love having this for solo lunches at home when I'm working.

**Serves 4**

8 heaped tablespoons Green
  Sauce (page 40)
1 litre (34 fl oz/4¼ cups)
  vegetable or chicken stock
150 g (5½ oz) small pasta
  shapes, such as ditalini or
  farfalline (optional)
350 g (12 oz) green vegetables of
  choice, such as mangetout
  (snow peas), frozen peas or
  broad (fava) beans, broccoli,
  asparagus or green beans,
  chopped into bite-sized pieces
ricotta or Parmesan, grated,
  to serve
sea salt and freshly ground
  black pepper

Put 2 heaped tablespoons of the green sauce into the bottom of four bowls.

Heat the stock in a saucepan until boiling, then season with salt and pepper and add the pasta, if using. Boil for 8–10 minutes (this may differ depending on your pasta), adding the green vegetables for the last 2 minutes until just cooked.

Ladle the stock and vegetables into each bowl, allowing the green paste to mix with the hot stock. Serve with a spoonful of ricotta or gratings of Parmesan.

# Green Oil for Everything

I do a lot of recipe testing, and it's an amazing job, but sometimes I just want to curl up on the sofa with something simple but really fresh and delicious that takes 10 minutes and very, very little effort to make. This sauce fits the bill, and it can be stored in the refrigerator ready to be tossed with any vegetable, poured over any meat, fish or eggs, or served with sticky rice or noodles. I particularly like to toss some of the sauce through noodles with some cucumber and shredded chicken for a simple dinner. It's the best thing to have in the refrigerator!

**Serves 2**

50 g (1¾ oz) or large handful of coriander (cilantro), leaves roughly chopped
bunch of spring onions (scallions), trimmed and thinly sliced
3 cm (1¼ inch) piece of fresh root ginger, peeled and finely chopped
small pinch of chilli (hot pepper) flakes (optional)
zest and juice of 1 lime
100 ml (3½ fl oz/scant ½ cup) vegetable oil
4 garlic cloves, very thinly sliced
1 heaped tablespoon white sesame seeds, toasted
1 tablespoon maple syrup, honey or caster (superfine) sugar
1 tablespoon light soy sauce
2 tablespoons toasted sesame oil (optional)
pinch of sea salt

Put the coriander, spring onions, ginger, chilli flakes, if using, and lime zest into a heatproof bowl.

Put the oil into a small frying pan (skillet) or saucepan, then add the garlic and sesame seeds. Place the pan over a medium heat and cook slowly for 5–7 minutes until the garlic is just golden and crisp. Remove from the heat, and pour into the bowl with the coriander. Add lime juice, maple syrup, soy sauce and the sesame oil, if using.

Transfer to a jar with a little more oil to cover the top. This will keep in the refrigerator for a week.

# PICKLES AND MARI- NADES

# BASIC PICKLE

A basic pickle brine is a very simple formula – three parts water, two parts vinegar, one part sugar and half salt. I've made a big batch in the recipe below, but feel free to halve or quarter it – just make sure the liquid is completley covering the fruit or vegetable.

Most of us love pickles, whether it's the gherkin (dill pickle) in a burger or the piccalilli in a cheese sandwich, and when you get that craving for something pickled, it's hard to avoid. Even if you think you don't like pickled things, the chances are that something you love has a vinegary, sharp element to it, as this is what balances out rich flavours. This is why I highly recommend adding a pickled item to your next cheese toastie (grilled cheese sandwich), or indeed anything that is high in fat.

Pickling is also one of the oldest and best ways to preserve things, so if you've bought a kilo of carrots and know you won't be able to use them all fresh, pickle a few! I hope I've made your mouth water a bit and you'll be tempted to pickle just one thing.

**Makes 500 ml (17 fl oz/ generous 2 cups)**

300 ml (10 fl oz/1¼ cups) boiling water
200 ml (7 fl oz/scant 1 cup) rice wine vinegar, white wine vinegar or apple cider vinegar
4 tablespoons caster (superfine) sugar
1 heaped teaspoon fine salt
spices and aromatics of choice (see opposite)
fruits or vegetables of choice (see opposite)

Put all the water, vinegar, sugar and salt into a saucepan and bring to the boil, then immediately remove from the heat. Add your chosen spices and aromatics while it's still hot as this will release any oils and intensify their flavours.

Either allow the brine to cool for a few minutes then pour over your fruits or vegetables while still hot (hot pickle) or leave to cool completely before pouring over (cold pickle).

Depending on what you pickle, store in the refrigerator for 1–4 weeks, ideally in a sterilised jar or container.

## What to pickle?

You can pickle almost any type of fruit or vegetable, either using hot or cold pickle brine. Things like squash, cauliflower or hardier vegetables like a hot pickle, whereas more delicate fruits and vegetables that need to retain their crunch, such as cucumbers, onions, celery or grapes, like a cold pickle. These are some of my favourites:

- Celery, finely sliced or roughly chopped

- Radishes, green parts trimmed and then either finely sliced, halved or left whole

- Red onions, peeled and finely sliced into half-moons

- Pears, cut into wedges

- Grapes, left whole

- Cauliflower, cut into florets

- Carrots, peeled and sliced however you want (I love them julienned for salad)

- Cucumber, thickly sliced

- Beetroot, peeled and sliced or chopped

- Chillies, left whole or sliced

- Rhubarb, finely sliced

## Spices and aromatics

- Fennel seeds

- Coriander seeds

- Turmeric

- Caraway seeds

- Cumin seeds

- Whole black peppercorns

- Mustard seeds

- Allspice berries

- Chilli flakes

- Bay leaves

# Marinated Peppers

We used to serve these peppers at the restaurant I worked at in Mallorca and they are infinitely delicious and versatile. We simply served them on their own with the very best extra virgin olive oil, but they're perfect with cured meats, cheese or any other cold bits you have, as well as steak or roast chicken. I use them for the Roast Vegetable and Tomato Salad on page 74. You can also use this marinade for olives, tinned artichokes, crumbled feta, anchovies, or even drained tinned tuna.

## Makes 1 x large jar

6–8 Romano or red (bell) peppers
125 ml (4 fl oz/½ cup) extra
   virgin olive oil
4 garlic cloves
1 teaspoon coriander seeds,
   toasted
1 teaspoon fennel seeds, toasted
few sprigs of thyme
1 lemon, quartered lengthwise
   and sliced
1 tablespoon red or white wine
   vinegar
sea salt and freshly ground
   black pepper

## Optional extras

1 heaped teaspoon mustard
   seeds, toasted
1 teaspoon dried oregano
few sprigs of rosemary
pared zest of 1 lemon

## To serve

basil leaves
salami or jamón
feta, broken into shards
Manchego, sliced
baguette
green salad

Preheat the oven to 220°C fan (475°F).

Place the peppers in a large, low-sided baking tray (pan) and roast in the oven for 30 minutes if using Romano peppers and 45 minutes if using regular bell peppers. The peppers should be collapsed and the skin blackened. Remove from the oven and transfer the peppers to a heatproof bowl, then tightly cover with a plate or cling film (plastic wrap). Leave to stand for 15 minutes. You want the peppers to steam so the skins easily come away from the flesh.

Lift the plate off and peel the skins from the peppers, discarding the seeds. Transfer to a jar or container of your choice along with the juices that have collected at the bottom of the bowl.

In a small saucepan over a medium heat, combine the oil with the whole garlic cloves, coriander and fennel seeds and thyme (along with any other optional extras). Slowly cook everything for 4–5 minutes until the garlic is starting to soften, then add the lemon slices and cook for a further 4–5 minutes. You don't want the oil to be bubbling, as the garlic will cook too fast. If it starts to bubble, just remove from the heat for 30 seconds before returning it to the heat to continue cooking. After 8–10 minutes, the garlic should be pale but completely soft on the inside. Stir in the vinegar with a pinch of salt and a few grinds of freshly ground black pepper.

Remove the pan from the heat and allow to cool for at least 20 minutes, then pour over the peppers. Either serve warm or allow to cool and store in the refrigerator for up to 2 weeks, keeping them covered in oil.

# Roast Vegetable and Tomato Salad and Hot Spiced Dressing

This is a really great barbecue dish that I regularly make every summer. The hot roast aubergine (eggplant), peppers and garlic tossed through the fresh tomato is such a satisfying dish to throw together. Everything sort of dresses itself in its own juices, making it ideal for mopping up with flatbreads. Plus, this tastes even better the next day.

This recipe is also great to make with the Marinated Peppers on page 72, and is equally as delicious served with feta, mozzarella, cream cheese or labneh. If tomatoes aren't in season, just add the tomato to roast with the other vegetables instead.

**Serves 2, or 4 as a side**

1 beef tomato or 2 vine tomatoes (ideally the best that summer can give you!), roughly chopped into 2 cm (¾ inch) chunks
1 garlic bulb, top sliced off
5 tablespoons extra virgin olive oil, plus extra for drizzling
1 large aubergine (eggplant)
1 red (bell) pepper or 2 Romano peppers
2 banana shallots, unpeeled and halved or 2 onions, unpeeled and quartered
50 g (1¾ oz) butter
½ teaspoon cumin
½ teaspoon chilli (hot pepper) flakes, plus extra to serve
½ teaspoon dried oregano
juice of ½ lemon
sea salt and freshly ground black pepper

**To serve**
200 g (7 oz) yogurt (optional)
flatbreads or sourdough

Preheat the oven to 200°C fan (425°F).

Put the tomato(es) into a bowl with a pinch of salt and give them a toss, then set aside.

Place the garlic in a piece of foil, drizzle with a little oil and sprinkle with salt, then wrap up.

Prick the aubergine all over with a knife and place it in a baking tray (pan) with the red pepper, shallots and garlic. Drizzle with 2 tablespoons of the olive oil and roast in the oven for 20 minutes.

After 20 minutes, remove the garlic and give everything a toss, then return to the oven for a further 15–20 minutes until the aubergine and pepper are completely softened and the skin of the pepper is slightly charred. If the pepper isn't ready, return to the oven for a final 5–10 minutes.

Remove from the oven and transfer everything to a heatproof bowl, then tightly cover with a plate or cling film (plastic wrap). Leave to stand for 15 minutes. You want the vegetables to steam so the skins easily come away from the flesh.

Take everything out of the bowl, leaving any juices behind. Split open the aubergine, then scoop out the insides and roughly chop them before adding them back into the bowl. Deseed the pepper and peel off its skin along with the skins of the shallots, then very roughly chop both and place back in the bowl. Season generously with salt and pepper.

Spread the yoghurt onto a plate, then pile the vegetables on top.

In a small saucepan, gently heat the butter with the remaining oil, cumin, chilli flakes and oregano. Squeeze the garlic out of its skin, then swirl it in the butter. Allow the butter and spices to bubble and foam for a minute, then remove from the heat, squeeze in the lemon juice and pour over the vegetables and yoghurt, if using. Sprinkle with extra chilli flakes, if you like, before serving.

# Charred Tomato Broth

This is the fresher, brothy sister to pasta and tomato sauce and it never ever gets old. Charring the tomatoes gives an intense depth to the soup. No one who eats it believes that it is this simple to make.

**Serves 4**

400 g (14 oz) cherry tomatoes
4 garlic cloves, peeled
2 tablespoons olive oil
1 tablespoon tomato purée
   (paste)
1 litre (34 fl oz/ 4¼ cups)
   water or vegetable stock
25 g (1 oz) basil, leaves picked,
   plus extra to serve
squeeze of lemon juice
150 g (5½ oz) fregola, rice,
   orzo, small pasta shapes or
   tinned beans
sea salt and freshly ground
   black pepper

**To serve**
knob of butter or extra virgin
   olive oil
chilli (hot pepper) flakes
grated Parmesan

Heat a dry, heavy-based frying pan (skillet) over a high heat. Once hot, add the tomatoes and char them all over for 6–10 minutes until blistered and softened (apologies for your smoky kitchen at this point!). A couple of minutes before the end, add the whole garlic cloves and char for 2 minutes, making sure not to burn them as they'll taste bitter.

Transfer the charred tomatoes and garlic to a large saucepan over a medium-high heat and add the olive oil and tomato purée. Fry for 2 minutes until the tomato purée has turned a darker red. Add the water or vegetable stock and bring to the boil, then reduce to a simmer and cook for 30–45 minutes (or up to 1 hour if you have time!).

Taste, then add the basil, lemon juice and a big pinch of salt and pepper. Once you're happy with the flavour, add the fregola, rice, pasta or beans and boil for 6–7 minutes until tender.

Serve with more basil, a knob of butter or a good glug of your best extra virgin olive oil, chilli flakes, Parmesan and a little more seasoning if it needs it.

# Roasted Squash and Crispy Greens with Pine Nut Butter and Feta

I have been fascinated by people's refrigerators while writing this book. I take a peek at what they've got and so often there's half a butternut squash going dry. This recipe is for that sad, forgotten squash. It's low effort but with an addictive flavour.

If you have a whole squash, roast it all as there are numerous things you can do with leftover roasted squash, such as adding it to the Green Soup on page 64, serving it with the Meatballs on page 125 or mashing it and stirring some through the Béchamel from page 134 for a creamy pasta sauce. It also makes the most of having the oven on.

**Serves 2, or 4 as a side**

½ butternut squash or pumpkin, or 2 sweet potatoes, cut into 5 cm (2 inch) chunks
3 tablespoons olive oil
100 g (3½ oz) kale or cavolo nero (lacinato kale), stalks removed
40 g (1½ oz) pine nuts (or flaked/slivered almonds or whole almonds, pecans or walnuts, roughly chopped)
30 g (1 oz) butter or 2 tablespoons extra virgin olive oil
1 tablespoon olive oil
10 sage leaves
juice of ½ lemon
100 g (3½ oz) feta, broken into shards
pinch of chilli (hot pepper) flakes
sea salt and freshly ground black pepper

Preheat the oven to 200°C fan (425°F).

Put the squash into a low-sided baking tray (pan) with 2 tablespoons of the oil and a generous pinch of salt. Rub the salt and oil all over the squash so it's evenly coated, then roast in the oven for 45 minutes until soft and deeply golden at the edges.

Put the kale into a bowl with the remaining oil and a small pinch of salt and scrunch the leaves until they have softened a little and are glossy.

Add the kale to the tray with the squash and roast for a further 5 minutes until the edges are a little crispy and the rest is just wilted and still bright green. I like the kale to still have some texture, so you don't need it to be fully wilted.

Put the pine nuts into a small frying pan (skillet) over a medium heat and toast them for 2 minutes until very lightly golden, shaking the pan to toss every so often. Add the butter and olive oil and cook for a minute until foaming, then add the sage leaves, letting the sage crisp and bubble in the butter for 2 minutes. Remove from the heat and squeeze in the lemon juice.

Serve wedges of the squash with a little pile of kale, a shard of feta, a drizzle of the pine nut butter, the crispy sage leaves, chilli flakes and a few cracks of black pepper.

# Poached Leeks with Sundried Tomatoes

I love making this at the start of the week as it gets better the longer the leeks are left in the flavoured oil. Once you've eaten the leeks, keep the oil and use it to marinate some crumbled feta or roasted peppers. I also like to use it as a base for dressings or for pouring over freshly cooked rice. The uses are endless.

**Serves 2, or 4 as a side**

8 sundried tomatoes, roughly
  chopped
4 tablespoons oil from the jar of
  sundried tomatoes
4 garlic cloves, peeled
1 tablespoon coriander seeds
4 tablespoons extra virgin olive oil
4 large leeks, trimmed and sliced
  into 5–10 cm (2–4 inch) lengths
300 ml (10 fl oz/1 ¼cups) water
2 tablespoons white wine vinegar
  or juice of 1 lemon
sea salt and freshly ground
  black pepper

**To serve**

250 g (9 oz) thick plain yoghurt,
  ricotta or cream cheese
2–4 slices of thickly cut
  sourdough bread, toasted
small handful of fresh dill or
  parsley leaves (optional)

Put the sundried tomatoes, sundried tomato oil, garlic cloves, coriander seeds and oil into a large, high-sided saucepan over a medium heat with a good pinch of salt and about five grinds of black pepper. Fry everything for about 2 minutes until the garlic is turning slightly golden. Add the leeks, making sure they sit in a single layer, then add the water (the water should just cover the leeks, so add a little more if necessary).

Bring to a simmer, then reduce the heat to low and cook for 15 minutes, turning the leeks over halfway through if they are thick, until the leeks are just soft and the water has reduced a little. Remove from the heat and allow to cool a little before adding the vinegar or lemon juice.

At this point, you can either allow the leeks to cool completely and store them in a container in the refrigerator to marinade and serve cold (they will keep for up to 1 week), or, while the leeks are still warm, dollop the yoghurt onto a plate or platter, then scoop the leeks out and place on top along with spoonfuls of the sundried tomato and garlic oil.

# Crushed Olive and Green Bean Salad

I couldn't not put this in the book. Green beans are my favourite vegetable – they're cruchy and fresh and I can eat them like chips (fries). This should be one of your staple side dish recipes. It goes with most things, packs so much flavour and you can chop and change most of the ingredients depending on what you have in the house. The olives can be swapped for capers or maybe cornichons (pickles). The green beans could be swapped for asparagus, helda beans or purple sprouting broccoli, or even just some leafy greens such as spring (collard) greens or hispi cabbage.

**Serves 4 as a side**

70 g (2½ oz) olives of choice, pitted (I like a mix of kalamata and green)
2 garlic cloves, thinly sliced
1 banana shallot, finely diced
pinch of chilli (hot pepper) flakes
3 tablespoons extra virgin olive oil
1 heaped tablespoon capers, drained and roughly chopped
small bunch of parsley, leaves finely chopped
1 tablespoon red or white wine vinegar, or the juice of ½ lemon
1 teaspoon honey or caster (superfine) sugar
400 g (14 oz) green beans, trimmed
small bunch of mint, leaves picked
1 ball of mozzarella, drained (optional)
sea salt

Using the bottom of a glass, crush the olives until they just split. Some might split in half and that's good – it's just to open them up so they catch all the hot dressing.

Put the garlic, shallots and chilli flakes into a cold frying pan (skillet) with the oil and a pinch of salt. Set over a medium heat and fry for 3–4 minutes until the garlic is very lightly golden and the shallot is just soft.

Add the olives, capers and parsley to the pan and swirl the pan for a minute, then remove from the heat and stir in the vinegar, honey and some more salt and pepper.

Bring a large saucepan of salted water to the boil and cook the green beans for 3 minutes, then drain and refresh under cold water. Toss the beans into the pan, then tip onto a plate or platter. Tear over the mint leaves and mozzarella, if using, then drizzle with any extra oil from the pan.

# MEAT

# AND

# FISH

# HOW TO ROAST A CHICKEN

Roast Chicken (pages 88–89)

Chicken Stock (page 93) with rice

Chicken Crackling (page 94) on Toast

One-pot Confit Onions and Herb-crusted Roast Chicken (pages 88–89)

The Chicken Bun (page 96)

Leftover Chicken Tacos (page 94)

# HOW TO ROAST A CHICKEN

One thing I always say about my job as a food stylist and writer is that I have roasted chicken in a lot of ways. Every chef and cook has their own method, which they swear by. I've roasted them upside down, I've slow-roasted them, I've marinated them in buttermilk, I've salted them overnight, I've salted them just before cooking, I've buttered them and I've oiled them. And to be honest, they've been delicious every time, because everyone who knows me knows I love roast chicken in any form. This is all to say that I am by no means the first (or will be the last) to write about roasting chicken, but it's something that feels so personal and deeply ingrained in my family culture that I can't not write a small essay about it.

My parents owned a restaurant for 20 years, from when I was five until I was about 25. They closed the restaurant every Sunday, without fail, so we could all get together and have a roast chicken (there were probably many other reasons to close, such as getting some sleep, but let's pretend it was just about the chicken, for the romance of it). It was one of the first things I learnt to cook, and Sundays feel strange when there isn't a chicken in the oven.

The main thing for me is the endless opportunities roasting a chicken provides. While I love the freshly roasted bird, I might love the things that come after it even more. A roast chicken represents one of the oldest ways of sustainable eating. The beauty and pure deliciousness of a great stock, for example, is just amazing. My dad is almost never not making a pot of stock. If he sees any scrap of bone, prawn shell or vegetable peel, there will be a stock bubbling that afternoon. When we go to a restaurant, he'll come home with bags of bones from the dinner, suckling pig and langoustine shells being the favourite. It causes a real problem with freezer space in the house. I can hear my mum now: 'Please, no more stock!'

Well, now it's my time to implore you: please, please keep the carcass from this roast chicken to make stock (page 93), which will give you the best meals for a whole week.

Cut off the string that's wrapped around the chicken legs, then lightly salt the chicken all over, seasoning from a height and turning the chicken to ensure an even, complete coverage. This ensures a moist, well-seasoned chicken. The salt will draw out the moisture from the skin as well as seasoning it, giving you the crispiest skin possible. At this point, you can refrigerate the chicken for 1 hour or overnight to get the best results but I never have the time or patience, so I set it aside for 30–40 minutes to bring it to room temperature.

**Serves 4**

1.5–2 kg (3 lb 5 oz–4 lb 8 oz)
  good-quality chicken
1 tablespoon fine salt
2 tablespoons olive oil
small handful of thyme sprigs
1 lemon, halved
2–4 garlic cloves, unpeeled and
  lightly crushed

**For the gravy (optional)**

125 ml (4 fl oz/½ cup) white wine
100 ml (3½ fl oz/scant ½ cup)
  water
1 x 400 g (7 oz) tin of lentils or
  white beans (optional)
20 g (¾ oz) butter
small handful of parsley, leaves
  chopped

Preheat the oven to as hot as it will go, about 240°C fan (500°F). Place the chicken in a roasting tin (I use something that can be put on the hob afterwards to make gravy). Pour the oil over the chicken and massage it all over with your hands. The oil gives the chicken a little kickstart in the oven, so make sure you get it into every nook and cranny to achieve maximum crispness.

Put the thyme, lemon and garlic into the chicken cavity, then roast in the oven, legs at the back, for 30 minutes. Reduce the heat to 180°C fan (400°F), rotate the chicken and roast for another 15–25 minutes until golden and crisp and the juices from the leg run clear. (These timings will differ with the size of your chicken but remember it will continue to cook while it's resting. You're aiming for 70°C/158°F at the base of the breast, if you have a meat thermometer.)

Now, this is the important part – when you remove the chicken from the oven, let it rest for at least 20–30 minutes. This allows the meat juices to be reabsorbed and will give you a moist and delicious chicken. I like to lift the chicken up using tongs and tilt it to allow the juices from the cavity to drip into the pan. Once rested, transfer to a chopping board. To make a delicious gravy or side dish, place the pan over a medium heat and bubble the resting juices with the wine and water for 10 minutes. At this point, you can also add the lentils or beans with their juices. Just before the end, stir in the butter and parsley until glossy.

To carve the chicken, position it with the legs facing you. Slice three-quarters of the way down between the leg and breast, releasing the skin but not going through the bone. Then, with your hands, simply grab one leg at a time and gently snap them off. They should naturally break off at the socket. Transfer to a warmed plate or platter. Next, feel for the centre bone of the chicken and, using a sharp knife, slice down slightly to the left of the bone and slowly cut down while pulling away with your hands so that you're able to neatly cut the breast meat away from the bone. Turn the chicken around, then repeat with the other breast. Slice the breasts however you wish, then add to the platter. You'll now be left with the wings. Simply pull the wings away from the carcass, which will show you where the break in the bone is, then slice down the middle to easily release the wings. Pour over the gravy, if you made it, and serve.

# Chicken Stock

Making stock is probably the smartest way to reduce food waste. You can use any offcuts from herbs and vegetables, such as parsley, thyme or rosemary stalks, onions, leeks, spring onions (scallions), carrots, tomatoes, fennel, garlic and fresh ginger peel. I like to keep a container of all the bits I collect during the week, then make a big pot of stock on Sunday using my roast chicken carcass.

You don't even need to have roasted and eaten a chicken to make this – I regularly go to the butcher and ask for any chicken carcasses or wings they have. They'll mostly give them to you for free.

**Makes 2 litres (68 fl oz/8½ cups)**

1 (or more) chicken carcasses or 500 g (1 lb 2 oz) chicken wings
1–2 onions (or any offcuts)
water, to cover

**Mix-and-match aromatics**
1–2 carrots, or carrot peelings or ends
1–4 celery sticks, or celery offcuts
1 leek, or leek trimmings
3–6 garlic cloves
2 bay leaves
4 sprigs of thyme
2 sprigs of rosemary
small handful parsley, leaves or stalks
2 tomatoes or a handful of cherry tomatoes
black peppercorns

**Mix-and-match South East Asian-style aromatics**
2 lemongrass stalks
100 g (3½ oz) piece of fresh root ginger, roughly chopped
bunch of spring onions (scallions)
4–6 garlic cloves
2 star anise
1 tablespoon coriander seeds
2 teaspoons fennel seeds

First, if you like, you can roast the bones or chicken wings for a deeper flavour. Preheat the oven to 200°C fan (425°F) and roast the bones or wings in a roasting tin for 30 minutes until golden.

Put the bones into a large saucepan, along with your aromatics of choice. Bring to the boil, then cover with a scrunched up piece of baking parchment and a lid. Reduce to a very low simmer and cook for a minimum of 2 hours, or up to 24 hours, then turn off the heat and allow to cool to room temperature before draining through a sieve into another pan.

I like to transfer the whole pot to the oven at this stage and cook the stock for a further 4–6 hours at 120°C fan (275°F) to make the best and clearest stock, but this is totally optional.

Allow to cool completely before storing in the fridge or freezer – Decant the finished stock into a container (or containers) and allow to cool completely before storing in the refrigerator or freezer until needed. It will keep for 4–6 days in the refrigerator and 6 months in the freezer.

# Leftover Chicken Tacos

These are delicious even if you don't have leftover chicken. I make them from scratch at home by roasting some chicken legs or thighs at 200°C fan (425°F), with the onions and spices, for 35 minutes, then stripping the meat and tossing with the roasting juices.

## Serves 4

½ teaspoon coriander seeds
½ teaspoon cumin seeds
1 tablespoon chipotle paste
3 tablespoons vegetable oil, plus extra as needed
2 onions, thinly sliced
2 garlic cloves, grated
350 g (12 oz) leftover cooked chicken (pages 88–89)
100 ml (3½ fl oz/scant ½ cup) water
sea salt

## To serve

1 onion
¼ white cabbage, very thinly shredded
juice of 2 limes, plus 2 limes to serve
8 medium or 12 small tortillas
a few tablespoons of pickled jalapeños or 2 fresh, thinly sliced

Toast the coriander and cumin seeds in a dry frying pan (skillet) until fragrant, then pour into a pestle and mortar and coarsely grind. Add the chipotle paste and a glug of vegetable oil and mix.

Heat the oil in a large saucepan or casserole dish (Dutch oven) over a medium heat. Add the onions with a pinch of salt and gently fry for 20 minutes, adding more oil if you need to until the onions are really soft and slightly caramelised. Put some time into cooking the onions as this is such an essential part of the dish. The more love you give the onions, the better it will taste. Stir in the garlic and fry for a further 2–3 minutes. Add the chicken and chipotle mixture and continue to fry for a minute before adding the water. Allow to bubble and thicken up for 5 minutes, then turn off the heat.

Peel the onion and then use a vegetable peeler to peel the flesh from the root end, creating very thin layers of onion (yes, I saw this on Instagram like the rest of us and love it – no need for a scary mandoline!). Place the onions in a bowl with the cabbage, add the lime juice and a pinch of salt, then scrunch everything together with your hands.

Warm the tortillas in a hot, dry pan or directly over a gas flame for a few seconds on each side, then stack on a plate. Serve the chicken and cabbage salad with the tortillas and jalapeños, allowing everyone to help themselves.

## Chicken Crackling

If you have leftover chicken skin, I urge you to make some crispy skin to top the tacos with. Lay the skin as flat as you can in a large frying pan, then drizzle in 1 tablespoon oil. Place a layer of baking parchment on top, followed by something heavy to weigh it down, such as a big saucepan. Fry over a medium-low heat for 4–5 minutes, then lift the weight and turn the skin over and fry for a further 2–3 minutes until completely crisp. Crunch up the skin and sprinkle over the tacos. See the grid image for inspiration!

# The Chicken Bun

I used to work at a beachside restaurant in Mallorca called Patiki and we served something very similar to this and everyone went MAD for it (I think it's still on the menu). It's a reminder of how great it is to have leftover chicken in the refrigerator.

Personally, I love celery and I think it's a key part of this recipe, providing a delicious crunch, but feel free to replace it with cucumber if it's not your thing. I'd recommend using one of the flavoured aiolis from pages 160–61 for this (particularly the Parmesan and black pepper one) or even adding a tablespoon of curry powder and a few raisins to make it more of a coronation chicken bun. It's also great as a simple salad if you'd rather not have the bun. Shred up a load of lettuce, then toss with the chicken mixture.

**Makes 2 buns**

250 g (9 oz) leftover cooked
   chicken, shredded
2½ heaped tablespoons
   mayonnaise or Aioli (see
   page 158)
juice of ½ lemon
1 teaspoon mustard, plus extra
   to serve
1 celery stick, finely chopped
small handful of fresh herbs, such
   as parsley, dill, chives or tarragon,
   leaves picked and finely chopped
4 cornichons or 1 large gherkin
   (dill pickle), finely chopped, plus
   extra to serve
sea salt and freshly ground
   black pepper

**To serve**
2 brioche burger buns (or any
   bread or buns you like), halved
a few lettuce leaves of your
   choice (I like Little Gem; optional)

Combine all the ingredients in a bowl to create a creamy mixture. Taste and add more lemon juice, mustard, pickles or herbs if you want.

Toast the halved buns in a dry frying pan (skillet) over a high heat until lightly golden, then pile on a few heaped tablespoons of the chicken mixture. Slice a few extra gherkins and drape them on top, add a few lettuce leaves, if using, then sandwich with the top bun and enjoy!

# Chicken, Tomatoes and Olives

This is a perfect one-pot comfort meal that uses mostly storecupboard ingredients and which gives the best leftovers. You can use any olives you like and mix and match them with anything else that's lingering in jars, such as capers or anchovies. I also add a few small new potatoes to the tray with the tomatoes at the start, or even stir in a drained jar of beans at the end. It's important to take the chicken out of the refrigerator 30 minutes before you're going to roast it, as this helps to create a perfectly roasted chicken.

**Serves 4**

500 g (1 lb 2 oz) vine tomatoes or halved/quartered large tomatoes
6 sundried tomatoes, roughly chopped
3 tablespoons oil from the jar of sundried tomatoes
2 tablespoons olives (any type), drained
6 garlic cloves, peeled
1.6 kg (3 lb 8 oz) chicken, at room temperature
2 tablespoons olive oil
1 lemon, halved
sea salt and freshly ground black pepper
mashed potatoes, brown rice or bread, to serve

Preheat the oven to as hot as it will go, about 240°C fan (500°F).

Put the tomatoes, sundried tomatoes, sundried tomato oil, olives and garlic into a 20 x 30 cm (8 x 12 inch) roasting tin, then place the chicken on top, making sure the tomatoes are positioned around the chicken and not underneath. Put one half of the lemon into the chicken cavity.

Drizzle the oil over the chicken and use your hands to rub it in. Season generously all over with salt and pepper.

Roast in the oven for 20 minutes, then reduce the heat to 180°C fan (425°F) and roast for a further 25–35 minutes until the skin is golden and crispy and the juices from the leg run clear. Remove from the oven and leave to rest in the tin for 20 minutes. Sometimes I like to remove the legs from the chicken and place them back into the oven in the tin to get extra crispy skin.

Carve the chicken, then place the pieces back into the tin for lazy serving, or alternatively, spoon the tomato and olive mixture onto a platter and place the chicken on top. Squeeze over the remaining lemon half before serving with mashed potatoes, brown rice or bread.

# One-pot Confit Onions and Herb-crusted Roast Chicken

This recipe was one of the last that I wrote for the book. It is probably what I cook the most at home, but in my head it was almost too simple to write a recipe for. It cooks in one pot and requires very few ingredients, all of which are easily interchangeable. The butter (lima) beans can be swapped for cannellini, chickpeas (garbanzo beans) or tinned lentils. The courgettes (zucchini) can be swapped for any number of things, too, such as 250 g (9 oz) cherry tomatoes (add these with the onions at the start), any leafy green such as kale, spinach, cavolo nero (lacinato kale) or even 100 g (3½ oz) frozen peas (add these right at the end for the last minute).

**Serves 4**

1.5–1.8 kg (3 lb 5 oz–4 lb) chicken
2 teaspoons fine sea salt
2 onions, thickly sliced
4 garlic cloves, peeled but left whole
2 teaspoons fennel seeds
4 tablespoons olive oil
60 g (2 oz) butter
1 lemon, halved
100 ml (3½ fl oz/scant ½ cup) white wine or water
1 teaspoon dried oregano
1 courgette (zucchini), sliced into 5 mm (¼ inch) rounds
2 x 400 g (14 oz) tins or jars of butter (lima) beans or 600 g (1 lb 5 oz) Beans for the Week (page 15)
sea salt freshly ground black pepper
Parmesan, to serve (optional)

Preheat the oven to as high as it will go (about 240°C fan/500°F).

Season the chicken all over with the salt, then set aside at room temperature for 30 minutes. One rested, dab the chicken with paper towels to remove any moisture that has come to the surface.

Put the onions and garlic into an ovenproof casserole dish (Dutch oven) or high-sided pan large enough to fit the chicken. Season with salt and sprinkle over half the fennel seeds, then drizzle with 3 tablespoons of the olive oil and give everything a good scrunch and mix so the onions are evenly coated. Dot around the butter, then lay the chicken on top.

Stuff the cavity of the chicken with half the lemon, then drizzle with the remaining olive oil. Rub the oil all over the chicken so that all the skin is covered. Roast in the oven for 25 minutes. Then remove the chicken from the oven and turn down the heat to 190°C fan (400°F). Pour the white wine or water around the chicken, then sprinkle over the remaining fennel seeds along with the oregano. Return to the oven for a further 25–30 minutes until the chicken is golden and cooked through and the onions are really soft, sitting in a layer of the chicken juices. Remove the chicken from the pan and transfer to a plate to rest.

Being careful not to burn yourself, place the pan with the onions over a medium heat and add the courgette. Cook for 5 minutes before tipping in the beans with half their juices. Let everything bubble away for a further 5 minutes, then add the juice and zest of the remaining lemon half, plus a generous amount of freshly ground black pepper.

Carve the chicken and place on a platter with the resting juices, then serve with the beans and a chunk of Parmesan for grating over.

# Roast Chicken, Spiced Spinach and Yoghurt

I really love saag aloo and I often crave it, so I created this simple and delicious one-pan dinner inspired by those flavours. This is not at all like an authentic saag aloo, it's my own version. You can use any spices you have in the cupboard here. I've also made this with chicken thighs by frying them skin-side down for 5–10 minutes until golden and crisp, then roasting in the oven for 25–35 minutes until cooked through. Then continue as instructed.

**Serves 4**

1 x 1.5-2 kg (3 lb 5 oz–4 lb 8 oz) good quality whole chicken OR 4-6 legs or 8 thighs (see intro), or 200–250 g (7 oz) leftover chicken (page 89)
1 tablespoons of vegetable oil
2 medium onions, peeled and finely sliced
1 teaspoon ground cumin
1 teaspoon mustard seeds
½ teaspoon turmeric
A pinch of chilli flakes
3 cm (1¼ inch) piece of ginger, peeled and finely grated
4 garlic cloves
400 g (14 oz) spinach

**To serve**

A few heaped tablespoons of yogurt
1 fresh green chilli, finely sliced (optional)

Preheat the oven to 240°C fan (475°F).

Season the chicken all over with salt, then set aside to rest for 30 minutes.

Place the chicken into an ovenproof frying pan (skillet), low-sided casserole dish (Dutch oven) or cast-iron pan. Pour the oil over the chicken and massage it in with your hands. The oil will give the chicken a little kickstart in the oven, so give it some love and attention and get the oil into every nook and cranny to achieve maximum crispness.

Roast in the oven, legs at the back, for 30 minutes. After this time, reduce the heat to 180°C fan (400°F), then rotate the chicken and roast for a further 10–25 minutes until golden and crisp all over and the juices from the leg run clear. (If you have a meat thermometer, you're aiming for 70°C/158°F at the base of the breast.)

Remove the pan from the oven, then lift out the chicken and set aside on a plate to rest.

Put the pan back over a medium heat and add the onions with a pinch of salt, tossing them in the chicken fat in the pan. Very slowly fry the onions for 10–15 minutes, stirring every so often until they are very, very soft and caramelised. If they start to fry too quickly, just turn down the heat and add a splash of water. Add the cumin, mustard seeds, turmeric, chilli flakes, ginger and garlic and fry for a further 5 minutes.

Add the spinach a handful at a time, mixing it into the onions as you go and letting it wilt with each batch. Let this cook down for a further 4–5 minutes until the spinach has soaked up all the flavours. Squeeze in the lemon juice and add a few grinds of black pepper, then taste.

Lay the chicken back on top of the spinach and serve to the table with the yoghurt and chilli.

# Garlic, Ginger and Sesame Oil Prawns

This combines my love for garlic prawns and chilli oil in one recipe. If you prefer the more classic garlic prawns, use the same method but leave out the ginger and sesame seeds and replace them with parsley and paprika.

**Serves 2**

200 g (7 oz) shelled raw king
  prawns (jumbo shrimp)
1 lime
100 ml (3½ fl oz/scant ½ cup)
  extra virgin olive oil
4 garlic cloves, sliced into 5 mm
  (¼ inch) slices
3 cm (1¼ inch) piece of fresh
  root ginger, peeled and sliced
  into 5 mm (¼ inch) slices
2 tablespoons white sesame seeds
small pinch of chilli (hot pepper)
  flakes (optional)
sea salt

**To serve**
few spring onions (scallions),
  thinly sliced
sticky rice or bread

Dry the prawns with paper towels (you don't want any water going into the hot oil), then season with salt and set aside.

Using a vegetable peeler, peel 4–5 strips of zest from the lime.

Pour the oil into a cold frying pan (skillet) and add the garlic, ginger, lime peel, sesame seeds and chilli flakes. You want the oil to be cold when you add the garlic so that it heats up with the oil and doesn't burn.

Place the pan over a medium-high heat and once the garlic starts to lightly sizzle (about 30 seconds), add the prawns and let it all sizzle together for 1–2 minutes until the prawns are light pink. Remove from the heat and let them continue to cook in the residual heat for 1 minute.

Serve with the spring onions and sticky rice or bread to soak up all the delicious oil.

# Poached Fish in End-of-Herbs Oil

This recipe is very versatile and it is a great way to demonstrate how easy it can be to pack something simple with flavour. I would recommend going to the fish counter or fishmonger for your fish, because the meatier the fish is, the more delicious this will be. It's really delicious served with boiled new potatoes and seasonal greens.

I have quite a neat steamer that sits on top of my frying pan (skillet) with a lid, so it's really easy to poach, but I understand that most people might not have this, so I have opted to include the most universal method below. However, if you do have a steamer like this, use it! Place the fish on a piece of baking parchment on the steamer and season with salt. Add 250 ml (8 fl oz/1 cup) water to the pan and bring to a simmer, then place the steamer on top, cover with the lid and steam for 8 minutes until the cod is just flaky to the touch.

I suggest using skin-on fish as it will help keep the piece of fish together while it cooks, but don't worry if you have skinless fish – you'll just have to be more careful when you lift the fish out of the water.

**Serves 2**

50 g (1¾ oz) parsley leaves, basil leaves and dill, plus extra to serve
2 garlic cloves
4 tablespoons extra virgin olive oil
500 ml (17 fl oz/generous 2 cups) vegetable stock or water
1 lemon
300 g (10½ oz) meaty white fish fillet, such as cod, hake or halibut (or use 2 x 150 g/5½ oz fillets)
1 tablespoon capers, drained
sea salt and freshly ground black pepper

Combine the herbs, garlic, oil and some salt and pepper in a food processor and blend for 1 minute until you have a vibrant green oil.

Pour the stock or water into a small frying pan (skillet) and add a generous pinch of salt. Use a vegetable peeler to peel the zest from the lemon and add that, too. The liquid should come just under three-quarters of the way up the pan, so add a little more if needed. Bring the water to the boil, then reduce to a very gentle simmer. Gently lower in the fish, then either cover with a lid or a scrunched up piece of baking parchment. Poach the fish for about 8 minutes until just cooked and flaky to the touch.

Carefully lift the fish out of the poaching water and place on a serving plate. Pour the oil over the fish and serve immediately with extra lemon juice, herbs, the capers and salt and pepper.

# Steak with Smash Burger Onions and Pickled Onion Chimichurri

I'm not really a burger girl, unless it's a smash burger, with those thin and jammy crispy onions, an intensely crisp but soft beef patty and a few pickles. Simple is best! So, when it comes to this steak, I want those same addictive flavours. I do this by using the steak cooking juices to cook the onions, then serving it all with a pickle-packed salsa. The point of the salsa is to use what you've got at home, so if you don't have (or don't like) celery or cucumber, simply leave them out. You just want a sharp salsa to break up the richness of the steak.

It's important to take the steak out of the refrigerator 30–40 minutes before you want to cook so that it is at room temperature. This will give you a more evenly cooked and less tough steak.

**Serves 2**

1 large onion
400 g (14 oz) rib eye, sirloin
   (strip) or bavette (flank) steak
   (ideally around 3 cm/1½ inches
   thick), at room temperature
2 tablespoons olive oil
20 g (¾ oz) butter
sea salt and freshly ground
   black pepper
mashed potatoes, to serve
(optional)

**For the pickle chimichurri**
1 celery stick, finely diced (plus
   a few leaves if you have them)
¼ cucumber, finely diced
6–8 small pickled onions, halved
   or roughly chopped, plus 2
   tablespoons pickle liquid
4–6 cornichons or 2 tablespoons
   capers
small handful of parsley, leaves
   finely chopped
small handful of chives, finely
   chopped
pinch of chilli (hot pepper) flakes
1 tablespoon capers, drained
zest and juice of 1 lemon

Halve the onion and thinly slice one half, then finely dice the other half. Put the diced onion into a bowl and stir in the rest of the pickle chimichurri ingredients.

Heat a heavy-based frying pan (skillet) over a high heat until smoking hot. While it's heating up, heavily season the steak on both sides and rub with the oil.

Add the steak to the hot pan. If it has a ridge of fat on one side, hold it in the pan fat-side down and cook for about 4 minutes until the fat is deeply golden and has rendered down.

Flip the steak onto the flat side and cook for 3–5 minutes on each side for medium-rare. This timing will depend on the thickness of your steak – this is why I suggest using a nice fat steak, as you can leave it on the heat for longer on each side to get a deeper colour and therefore a better flavour. In the last few minutes, add the butter and, once melted, baste the steak.

Remove the steak from the pan and set aside to rest. Turn the heat down to medium and add the sliced onions and a pinch of salt, then cook, stirring regularly, for about 5 minutes until the onions are jammy and golden. Spoon the onions onto a platter.

Slice the steak into thin strips, then transfer to a platter with the onions and spoon over the chimichurri.

# BREAD

# CRISPY BREAD-CRUMBS TO TOP ALMOST ANYTHING

Crispy Breadcrumbs (page 114) with lettuce tossed in Green Goddess Dressing (page 60)

Creamy Corn Pasta (page 141)

Schnitzel with Curry Mayo (page 119)

Creamy Aubergine Puddle with Courgettes and Almond Breadcrumbs (page 116)

Crispy Breadcrumbs (page 114) with feta, cucumbers, olives, spring onions (scallions) and parsley

Salted Sesame Caramelised Breadcrumbs with Ice Cream and Olive Oil (page 122)

# CRISPY BREADCRUMBS TO TOP ALMOST ANYTHING

We waste an unimaginable amount of bread in the world, and I can almost guarantee that you've got a chunk of bread in the house somewhere going stale. This bit of bread you have can make so many delicious things.

All you need to do is blitz up the bread you have (this can be anything from sourdough to plain white bread, to rye bread, crumpets or bagels), then place half of it into a bag or container to freeze and use as fresh breadcrumbs and spread the other half out on a baking sheet and allow to dry for 24 hours. Then transfer the dried breadcrumbs to a jar and use them for all sorts of things. See below for one versatile way to use your homemade breadcrumbs.

**Makes 100 g (3½ oz)**

50 ml (1¾ fl oz/3½ tablespoons) olive oil
100 g (3½ oz) fresh or dried homemade breadcrumbs
1 garlic clove, finely grated or chopped
zest of 1 lemon
sea salt and freshly ground black pepper

**Optional extras**
30 g (1 oz/⅓ cup) flaked (slivered) almonds
2 tablespoons drained capers
2 tablespoons white sesame seeds
handful fresh thyme

Heat the oil in a frying pan (skillet) over a medium-high heat. Add the breadcrumbs (and almonds, capers or sesame seeds and thyme, if using), tossing them in the oil so that they are evenly coated. Add more oil If you feel they need it.

Fry for 4–6 minutes until every grain is golden and crisp. Add the garlic to fry for the final minute, then remove from the heat and add the lemon zest.

Season with salt and pepper, then use to sprinkle over salads, pastas or vegetables for added flavour and texture.

# Creamy Aubergine Puddle with Courgettes and Almond Breadcrumbs

I'm obsessed with textures. When I'm writing recipes, I'll often be led by the textures of the dish – I will consider what texture is still needed, and whether that's crispy, crunchy, creamy or otherwise. This has it all – layers of really simple flavours, combined to create the perfect mouthful. Leave the yoghurt and Parmesan out if you want this to be vegan.

This creamy aubergine (eggplant) base can be used as a dip or it can be a be topped with any green vegetables such as asparagus, peas, broad (fava) beans, green beans, broccoli, cabbage, etc.

**Serves 2**

2 aubergines (eggplants)
6 garlic cloves, unpeeled
juice of ½ lemon
2 heaped tablespoons Greek or
    plain yoghurt
2 tablespoons tahini
20 g (¾ oz) Parmesan, grated
sea salt and freshly ground
    black pepper

**For the almond breadcrumbs**

50 g (1¾ oz/scant ⅔ cup)
    fresh breadcrumbs (make your
    own from any stale bread, such
    as sourdough, rye bread or even
    crumpets)
4 tablespoons extra virgin olive oil
30 g (1 oz) flaked (slivered)
    almonds or finely chopped whole
    almonds

**For the courgettes**

2 large or 3 small courgettes
    (zucchini), sliced into 1 cm
    (½ inch) rounds
2 tablespoons extra virgin olive oil
juice of ½ lemon
small handful of basil leaves,
    parsley leaves or dill (or a mixture)

Preheat the oven to 220°C fan (475°F).

Pierce the aubergines a few times with a knife and place on a baking tray (pan). Wrap the garlic in foil and add to the same tray. Roast in the oven for 35 minutes until the aubergine is completely collapsed and soft in the middle.

Remove from the oven, unwrap the garlic and allow to cool for 10 minutes, then squeeze the garlic from their skins into a food processor. Slice the aubergines in half and scoop out the flesh into the food processor too. Add remaining ingredients, along with a pinch of salt and a generous few grinds of black pepper. Blend for 1 minute until smooth and creamy.

Next, make the almond breadcrumbs. If making your own breadcrumbs, simply tear the bread up into small pieces and blitz in a food processor for 30 seconds.

Heat the oil in a small frying pan (skillet) over a medium heat and gently fry the breadcrumbs and almonds for 5 minutes until golden and crisp.

Bring a large saucepan of salted water to boil and cook the courgettes for 4 minutes until just cooked. Drain, then add back into the pan with the oil, lemon juice and herbs. Season with salt and pepper and toss to combine.

Dollop the aubergine cream onto a large plate or platter, then pile on the courgettes and scatter over the breadcrumbs to serve.

# All Greens Greek Salad

In the height of summer when courgettes are EVERYWHERE, I find myself trying to use a courgette in everything. They are amazing braised (please make the One-pot Confit Onions and Herb-crusted Roast Chicken on page 100 for this) but also delicious eaten raw too. I made this as a picnic for my boyfriend and I to eat by the sea in Dublin and it was memorably good.

## Serves 2, or 4 as a side

1 medium or 2 small courgette, thinly sliced in to 5 mm (¼ in) rounds
½ a cucumber, thinly sliced in to 5 mm (¼ in) rounds
4 spring onions, finely sliced OR ½ red onion, halved and very finely sliced
a small bunch of parsley or basil or a mix, leaves picked
a few handfuls of pitted olives. I like kalamata for this but use any you like
200 g (7 oz) feta, sliced into thin shards

### For the dressing
juice and zest of ½ lemon
4 tablespoons of olive ioil
1 teaspoon of dried oregano, plus extra to serve
sea salt and freshly ground black pepper

### To serve
handful of Crispy Breadcrumbs (page 114)

Add the courgette, cucumber, spring onions, herbs and olives to a large bowl.

Pour in the dressing ingredients along with salt and pepper, to taste. Give it a good stir so it's all coated, then pile onto plates.

Add the shards of feta on top, then sprinkle with a little more dried oregano to finish, along with a handful of breadcrumbs.

# Schnitzel with Curry Mayo

I was hesitant about putting this in the book, but it's definitely one of my favourite things to eat and a great way to use breadcrumbs. I've added sesame seeds to the breadcrumbs here and served it with a curried mayo for an extra kick of flavour, but they are by no means essential.

Eat with a simple salad, or I'd also recommend serving it with my Crushed Olive and Green Bean Salad from page 82, pickled radishes from page 70.

**Serves 2–4**

4 skinless chicken breasts or
   turkey breast fillets
100 g (3½ oz/generous ¾ cup)
   plain (all-purpose) flour
2 eggs, beaten
100 g (3½ oz/1 cup) fresh or
   dried breadcrumbs
60 g (2 oz/generous ⅓ cup)
   white sesame seeds (optional)
150 ml (5 fl oz/scant ⅔ cup)
   vegetable oil
sea salt and freshly ground
   black pepper
chilli sauce of choice, to serve

**For the curried mayo**

50 g (1¾ oz) butter
2 teaspoons curry powder
4 tablespoons mayonnaise
zest and juice of 1 lime

First, make the curried mayo. Heat the butter in a small saucepan over a high heat until foaming, then add the curry powder. Swirl the pan and let it bubble for 30 seconds, then remove from the heat. Allow to cool for a few minutes, then pour three-quarters into a bowl and stir in the mayonnaise with half the lime juice. Pour over the remaining curry butter and set aside.

Place each chicken breast between two pieces of cling film (plastic wrap) or baking parchment, then, one at a time, bash them with a rolling pin to flatten to about 1 cm (½ inch) thick.

Put the flour into a bowl or shallow dish and season with a pinch of salt and pepper. Put eggs into another dish and the breadcrumbs and sesame seeds into a third. Set out an empty baking sheet to put the chicken on once breaded.

Dip each chicken breast into the flour, coating it all over by patting it into the meat. Shake off any excess, then dip into the egg mixture, again making sure every bit of the meat is coated. Finally, dip the chicken into the breadcrumb mixture, making sure every little bit is covered. Place the chicken on the baking sheet and repeat with the remaining breasts.

Heat the oil in a large frying pan (skillet) over a medium heat. You want the oil to be 1.5 cm (just over ½ inch) deep, so add a little more if needed. Once the oil is hot, add one of the chicken breasts and fry for 3 minutes on each side, basting with the oil until the crust is even and golden. Transfer to a plate lined with paper towels, then repeat with the remaining chicken.

Serve with the curry mayonnaise, pickled radishes, potatoes and a side of your choice, along with the remaining lime to squeeze over.

*(Images overleaf)*

# Salted Sesame Caramelised Breadcrumbs with Ice Cream and Olive Oil

OK, so if you're going to make anything in this book, make this. It's very addictive, and I love it! I suggest scaling up the recipe to make a load because I find myself sprinkling it on top of everything.

**Serves 4**

100 g (3½ oz) stale bread
70 g (2½ oz) salted butter
2 heaped teaspoons white
   sesame seeds
70 g (2½ oz) light brown soft
   sugar (or caster/superfine
   sugar)
pinch of flaky sea salt
ice cream, to serve (I like vanilla or
   chocolate for this)
extra virgin olive oil, to serve

Tear the bread into small chunks, then blitz in a food processor to make breadcrumbs.

Melt the butter in a frying pan over a medium-high heat until foaming. Add the breadcrumbs and sesame seeds and toss to coat in the butter. Fry for 5–8 minutes until the breadcrumbs are crisp.

Sprinkle in the sugar and stir to coat the breadcrumbs, then fry for a further 2 minutes. If it looks a bit dry, add in a little more butter. Pour onto a baking sheet and allow to cool.

Scoop the ice cream into bowls, then top with the breadcrumbs and a drizzle of extra virgin olive oil.

# Crispy Sesame Sausage Toasts

Want a sausage roll but don't want to turn the oven on? Have some bread and a sausage? Well, then this recipe is for you. I've made this version in the same way that you would make prawn toast (mashing the sausage meat with flavourings) but if you have a really well-flavoured sausage, just pat that onto toasted bread and fry it as is. These are also very good topped with cheese and grilled.

**Serves 2–4**

4–6 pork sausages
5 spring onions (scallions), finely
  chopped
15 g (½ oz) coriander (cilantro),
  stalks finely chopped
2 garlic cloves, grated
1 cm (½ inch) piece of fresh root
  ginger, grated
1 teaspoon light soy sauce
½ teaspoon runny honey
4 thick slices of bread (I use
  sourdough, but any would work)
3 tablespoons sesame seeds
(black or white or a mixture of
  both)
3 tablespoons vegetable oil
zest and juice of 1 lime
pinch of sea salt
chilli sauce of choice, to serve
  (optional)

Squeeze the sausage meat out of the casings into a bowl and add two-thirds of the spring onions, the chopped coriander stalks, garlic, ginger, soy sauce and honey. Mash together with a fork until well combined.

Toast the slices of bread, then lay them out on a board or large plate. Spread the sausage mixture evenly over the toast in a 5 mm (¼ inch) layer, then sprinkle with the sesame seeds.

Heat the oil in a large frying pan (skillet) over a medium heat and place the toasts sausage-side down into the pan to fry for 4–5 minutes until golden and crisp (you may have to do this in batches). Remove from the pan and transfer to a serving plate.

Combine the remaining spring onions with the coriander leaves, lime zest and juice and salt in a small bowl. Top each crispy sausage toast with a mound of the spring onion and coriander.

Eat immediately with your hands, dipping in chilli sauce if you like.

# The Lightest Meatballs

This is a base recipe for meatballs, using bread soaked in milk to ensure a supremely light result. They can be served with polenta, mashed potatoes, a simple dollop of yoghurt and flatbreads, or just as they are with boiled seasonal greens in olive oil, lemon juice and lots of black pepper. Top with a drizzle of the juices from the pan and a dollop of mustard – perfect.

They can be flavoured however you like. My favourite flavour combination is the one below, but I also love to make these with minced (ground) beef and lamb flavoured with cumin, za'atar and/or sumac, then served on yoghurt with some fresh mint. Ginger, garlic, spring onions (scallions) and chilli are a great combination too.

## Makes 16

500 g (1 lb 2 oz) minced (ground) beef or pork, or a mixture of the two

1 teaspoon sea salt

75 g (2½ oz) fresh white breadcrumbs or crustless white bread, such as sourdough, ciabatta or any white loaf, blitzed into breadcrumbs

75 ml (2½ fl oz/5 tablespoons) milk

2 garlic cloves, grated

handful of parsley, leaves finely chopped

1 egg, beaten

1 tablespoon dried oregano (optional)

1 teaspoon fennel seeds (optional)

20 g (¾ oz) Parmesan, grated (optional)

3 tablespoons olive oil

50 ml (1 ¾ fl oz/3½ tablespoons) white wine or water

Put the meat into a bowl with the salt and use your hands to mix together, then set aside to rest for 15 minutes.

In a separate bowl, combine the bread with the milk and leave to soak for 10 minutes.

Add the soaked bread and all the remaining ingredients, except the oil and wine, to the meat, then scrunch everything together with your hands until well combined. Divide into 16 balls (about 50 g/1¾ oz each) and place on a tray or plate, then refrigerate for 1 hour to firm up.

Heat the oil in a large frying pan (skillet) over a high heat and fry the meatballs in batches for 6–10 minutes until evenly golden on all sides.

Add all the meatballs snugly back into the pan and reduce the heat to low. Pour in the wine or water, cover with a lid and steam for 5–8 minutes until cooked through.

Remove from the heat and rest in the pan for 5 minutes before serving.

Is there anything better than a leftover meatball? Make double the quantity and freeze them if you like. They'll last for up to 6 months in the freezer, or a week in the refrigerator.

*(Images overleaf)*

The Lightest Meatballs (page 125) in broth with pasta and greens

The Lightest Meatballs (page 125)

The Lightest Meatballs (page 125) with mashed potato (page 44) and steamed greens

The Lightest Meatballs (page 125) served on bread with tomato sauce, mozzarella and basil

The Lightest Meatballs (page 125) in tomato sauce

The Lightest Meatballs (page 125) with rice, tahini and yogurt

# Sesame and Honey Wafer Toasts

You can make these toasts with however much bread you have left over, but sometimes I buy a loaf just to make a batch because they are so addictive! Just double the sesame and honey mixture according to how much you're making. I like to serve these with a chunk of cheese and some seasonal fruit.

**Makes 10–12 toasts**

240 g (8½ oz) stale bread (this works best with sourdough, rye bread, a seeded loaf or anything that can be sliced very thinly)
2 tablespoons white sesame seeds
5 tablespoons olive oil
3 tablespoons runny honey
pinch of flaky sea salt

**Optional extras**
1 teaspoon nigella seeds
1 tablespoon za'atar
1 teaspoon ground cinnamon

Preheat the oven to 160°C fan (350°F) and line two large baking sheets with baking parchment.

Slice the bread as thinly as you can – the thinner the slices are, the crisper and more delicate the toasts will be, so take your time, but don't worry if you get some half slices or they're not perfect.

In a small bowl, mix together the sesame seeds, olive oil, honey and sea salt, plus any optional extras you like.

Pour the sesame mixture over the bread and use your hands to rub it all over each slice until evenly coated.

Bake in the oven for 15–20 minutes until golden, then remove from the oven and leave to cool on the sheets. Store in an airtight container for up to 2 weeks.

# MILK,

# CHEESE

# AND

# DAIRY

# BÉCHAMEL SAUCE

Chunky Roast Leeks with a Blanket of Cheesy Béchamel (page 138)

Chunky Roast Cauliflower with a Blanket of Cheesy Béchamel (page 138)

Potatoes tossed in Parsley Sauce (page 137) and mustard

Cheese and Béchamel Toasts (page 134)

Creamy Corn Pasta (page 141)

Mum's Ham Cakes with Parsley Sauce (pages 46–47)

# BÉCHAMEL SAUCE

This might just be the key to… everything? Knowing how to make a béchamel sauce is one of the most important parts of being a home cook. After you've mastered this, you can make lasagne, mac and cheese, parsley sauce, cheese sauce, moussaka, fish pie, chicken pie and, of course, the recipes on the following pages.

**Makes 550 ml (19 fl oz/ 2⅓ cups)**

500 ml (17 fl oz/generous
    2 cups) milk
50 g (1¾ oz) butter
50 g (1¾ oz/scant ½ cup) plain
    (all-purpose) flour
sea salt and freshly ground
    black pepper

Melt the butter in a large saucepan over a medium heat, then stir in the flour until it forms a paste (the roux). Cook, stirring, for 2 minutes to cook out the flour. If you don't, the béchamel will taste like flour.

Slowly add a quarter of the milk, stirring constantly. It will instantly thicken up as the flour soaks up the milk, but keep going, stirring all the time until you have a smooth paste. Add another quarter of the milk, continuing to stir. It will start to loosen up and look a bit more like a sauce. Repeat with the remaining milk. You should have a really silky but thick sauce. Finish with a generous pinch of salt and pepper.

## What to make next?

### Cheese sauce
Add two large handfuls of grated cheese of your choice to the hot sauce, then stir into pasta and bake in the oven or use it to layer a lasagne.

### Creamy green sauce for pasta
Stir in some Green Sauce (page 60) to make a creamy green sauce, then stir into pasta or use it to layer a lasagne.

### Quick chicken and spinach pie
Stir in leftover chicken or ham (or both), 200 g (7 oz) spinach, a handful of parsley or tarragon and 1 tablespoon Dijon mustard, then transfer to a dish and top with shop-bought puff pastry. Bake for 35 minutes at 200°C fan (425°F).

### Cheese and béchamel toasts
Dollop 6 tablespoons of leftover béchamel into a bowl with 3 finely chopped spring onions, a tablespoon of mustard and a large handful of grated hard cheese (Cheddar, Parmesan, manchego or comté). Mix, then spread onto toast. Place under the grill until golden and bubbling.

# Things with Parsley Sauce

My family loves parsley sauce – we eat it a lot, with a lot of different things because it just tastes so good. In the UK, the classic parsley sauce is a thinner, more gelatinous version served with pie and mash, but we love this creamier version poured over potatoes, green beans or with a slice of ham.

**Serves 2, or 4 as a side**

handful of parsley, leaves finely
  chopped
1 teaspoon Dijon mustard
juice of ½ lemon
½ x quantity Béchamel Sauce
  (page 134)
freshly ground black pepper

**To serve**
750 g (1 lb 10 oz) new potatoes
40 g (1½ oz) butter or 2
  tablespoons extra virgin olive oil
200 g (7 oz) fine green beans,
  broccoli, purple sprouting
  broccoli, helda beans or
  asparagus
sea salt

Stir the parsley, mustard and lemon juice into the hot béchamel sauce along with a generous pinch of black pepper. At this point, you can either use a hand-held blender or food processor to blend it and turn it a vibrant green, or just use it as it is.

Boil the potatoes for 8–12 minutes in a large saucepan of salted boiling water until tender, then drain and toss with half the butter or oil and season with salt and pepper. Boil the green beans for 2–3 minutes, then drain and toss with butter or oil and salt and pepper.

Pour the parsley sauce onto a large serving plate or platter and top with the boiled potatoes and green beans.

# Chunky Roast Vegetables with a Blanket of Cheesy Béchamel

There are, many, many ways you can make this recipe, switching out the vegetables with what's in season or in the house. Big chunks of celeriac (celery root), fennel, squash or even wedges of cabbage would be a great swap for the cauliflower. Instead of leeks you could use peeled and halved onions or shallots.

If you have any left over, I like to blitz it up and stir it through cooked pasta.

**Serves 4**

1 large cauliflower, large leaves removed or 6 leeks, tough outer leaves removed
2 onions, quartered (if making the cauliflower version)
3 tablespoons olive oil
150 g (5½ oz) grated cheese (you can use anything you have in the refrigerator, but I recommend 100 g/3½ oz Cheddar and 50 g/1¾ oz Gruyère, Comté, Parmesan or blue cheese), plus extra for sprinkling
1 x quantity Béchamel Sauce (page 134)
50 g (1¾ oz) fresh breadcrumbs, tossed in 1 tablespoon olive oil (optional)
sea salt and freshly ground black pepper

## For the cauliflower version
Preheat the oven to 220°C fan (475°F).

Cut the cauliflower into quarters and place in a large roasting tin with the onions. You want everything to fit quite snugly but also have a little space around each piece. Rub the oil all over the vegetables, season with salt and pepper and roast in the oven for 30 minutes until the tops of the cauliflower are a little charred and golden, and the onions are soft.

Meanwhile, stir the cheeses into the hot béchamel.

Remove the vegetables from the oven, pour the sauce over, then turn on the grill. Sprinkle with a little more cheese and the breadcrumbs, if using, and grill for 5–10 minutes until golden and bubbling.

## For the leek version
Preheat the oven to 220°C fan (475°F).

Slice the leeks into thick chunks and place in a large roasting tin. You want everything to fit quite snugly but also have a little space around each piece. Rub the oil all over the leeks and season with salt and pepper, then cover with foil and roast in the oven for 40–45 minutes until completely soft.

Meanwhile, stir the cheeses into the hot béchamel.

Remove the leeks from the oven, pour the sauce over, then turn on the grill. Sprinkle with a little more cheese and the breadcrumbs, if using, and grill for 5–8 minutes until golden and bubbling.

# Creamy Corn Pasta

I suppose this is a bit like a lazy version of a mac and cheese, but the corn gives it the extra crunch that I think mac and cheese needs. It uses three pans, which is very unlike me! Sorry about the extra washing up, but it only takes 15 minutes to make and is really delicious.

**Serves 2–3**

50 g (1¾ oz) stale bread or fresh breadcrumbs
2 corn on the cob, kernels sliced off or 1 x 350 g (12 oz) tin of sweetcorn
½ x quantity Béchamel Sauce (page 134)
30 g (1 oz) Parmesan, grated, plus extra to serve
30 g (1 oz) Cheddar, grated
200 g (7 oz) pasta of choice (my favourite for this is rigatoni or spaghetti)
2 tablespoons extra virgin olive oil
1 garlic clove, grated
zest of 1 lemon
sea salt and freshly ground black pepper
finely chopped chives and parsley, to serve (optional)

If making your own breadcrumbs, tear the bread up into small pieces and blitz in a food processor for 30 seconds.

Add half the corn to the hot béchamel sauce along with the cheeses and a good pinch of salt and pepper. Cook for 1 minute over a medium heat, then remove from the heat and set aside.

Cook the pasta in a large saucepan of salted boiling water according to the packet instructions.

Meanwhile, heat the oil in a frying pan (skillet) over a medium-high heat. Add the remaining corn and the breadcrumbs and stir to coat in the oil. Fry for 3–4 minutes, stirring regularly, until the breadcrumbs are lightly golden. Finally, add the garlic and lemon zest and fry for a further minute.

Before draining the pasta, scoop out a mugful of the pasta water and set aside. Drained the pasta, then transfer it back to the saucepan with the cheese sauce, along with a few splashes of the pasta water. Stir together until the sauce is lovely and glossy and has coated all the pasta.

Add a few more grinds of black pepper, then serve with the corn breadcrumbs, extra Parmesan and the herbs, if using.

# Soda Bread

**Makes 6 rolls or 1 large loaf**

450 g (1 lb/scant 3¼ cups) plain
  (all-purpose) flour, plus extra for
  dusting
2 teaspoons bicarbonate of soda
  (baking soda)
½ teaspoon sea salt
375 ml (12½ fl oz/generous
  1½ cups) buttermilk
butter, to serve

**Optional extras**

50 g (1¾ oz) grated hard cheese,
  such as Cheddar, Gruyère, Comté
  or Parmesan
1 garlic clove, grated
4 sprigs of rosemary or thyme
25 g (1 oz) chives or parsley, leaves
  finely chopped
1 green or red chilli, deseeded and
  finely chopped
pinch of chilli (hot pepper) flakes
1 fresh green chilli, chopped
handful of chopped dates, prunes,
  dried figs/cranberries, raisins,
  sultanas (golden raisins), walnuts,
  pecans or almonds

I've used plain (all-purpose) flour for this recipe as I think it's what most households will already have, but most traditional soda bread recipes use a mix of flours. If you have any wholemeal (whole-wheat) or spelt flour, use that to replace 150 g (5½ oz/scant 1¼cups) of the plain flour for additional flavour. This can, of course, be baked as one big soda bread instead of rolls if you prefer.

It's so easy to make your own buttermilk at home – it's just thickened, curdled milk, so all you need is milk and some vinegar or lemon juice. See opposite for a method if you want to try this out.

Preheat the oven to 190°C fan (400°F) and line a baking tray (pan) with baking parchment.

In a bowl, combine the flour, bicarbonate of soda and salt, plus any optional extras you like. Stir in the buttermilk until it forms a soft and shaggy dough.

Turn the dough out onto a lightly floured surface and gently knead for 1 minute – you don't need to really knead the dough as it doesn't have yeast, but you want to bring it all together to form a loose dough. With floured hands, divide the dough into six rough balls.

Carefully transfer the balls of dough to the prepared baking tray, leaving a 2 cm (¾ inch) gap between each one. Dust the rolls with a little flour, then use a sharp knife to score a deep cross (or whatever shape you like) onto the top of each one.

Bake in the oven for 15–18 minutes until risen, golden brown and hollow-sounding when tapped on the bottom.

Remove from the oven and allow to cool for at least 20 minutes, then serve warm or cold with loads of butter.

I've served mine here with 150 g (5½ oz) cream cheese mixed with 2 tablespoons chopped pickled chillies and a handful of finely chopped chives.

## Making your own buttermilk

Once you make your own buttermilk, you'll wonder why you ever bothered buying it. It's so simple and makes the fluffiest cakes, pancakes and bread as well as being a great marinade for meats.

350 ml (12 fl oz/1½ cups) whole (full-fat) milk
juice of 1 lemon or 2 tablespoons white wine vinegar

Pour the milk into a bowl or jug (pitcher), add the lemon juice or vinegar and set aside to thicken for 10 minutes.

# Double Cheese and Green Chilli Tart with Coriander and Lime Salsa

If you're making something that's rich with cheese or cream, it's important to have something to balance out the flavour. Here, I've used pickled chillies to cut through the cheese. If you don't like spice, I think you'll like this, as it's more about the tangy flavour. If you prefer not to add them to the base, then I recommend serving the finished tart with some pickles instead. You could also stir some pickled celery, radishes or cucumbers from page 70 into the salsa.

**Serves 4**

1 x 375 g (13¼ oz) sheet of puff
  pastry
2 eggs, beaten
200 g (7 oz) crème fraîche, ricotta
  or cream cheese
2 small or 1 large garlic clove, grated
120 g (4¼ oz) Cheddar,
  Manchego, Parmesan, Comté or
  Gruyère, grated
1 ball of mozzarella, torn
4 pickled green chillies or
  2 tablespoons pickled jalapeños,
  thinly sliced
sea salt and freshly ground
  black pepper

### For the coriander salsa

1 small onion or shallot, ½ small red
  onion or bunch of spring onions
  (scallions), thinly sliced
zest and juice of 1 lime
bunch of coriander (cilantro), leaves
  picked
small handful of chives, finely
  chopped
1 green chilli, thinly sliced

Preheat the oven to 180°C fan (400°F).

Unroll the pastry and place it on a baking sheet on the baking parchment it came with.

Lightly score a 2 cm (¾ inch) border around the pastry (making sure you don't go all the way through the pastry) ,then prick a few marks into the middle with a fork. Brush the border with a little of the beaten eggs, reserving the rest to add to the filling.

Bake the pastry base in the oven for 15 minutes until lightly golden, then remove from the oven and set aside. If the centre has puffed up a bit, just pat it down with the back of a fork or spoon.

In a bowl, combine all the remaining ingredients and season well.

Spread the mixture onto the pastry base inside the border, then bake in the oven for 20 minutes until golden and bubbling.

Meanwhile, make the coriander salsa. Combine the onion and lime zest and juice in a bowl with a pinch of salt and massage them with your hands so the onion is coated in the lime juice. Just before serving, toss the herbs and chilli into the limey onions, then pile on top or serve alongside the tart.

# 'Burrata' and Chilli Oil Dressed Tomatoes

If you don't know Clare Thompson (@5oclockapron on Instagram), then you should. I really love her recipes. She's very clever with what she creates, and one of those clever ideas is her cheat's burrata. I use it for the base of a lot of things.

For this recipe, all I ask is that you get the best tomatoes you can, because the more delicious the tomato, the more delicious the whole dish will be.

**Serves 2**

1 ball of mozzarella, drained
3 tablespoons crème fraîche
2–3 large tomatoes, chopped into large chunks
1–2 tablespoons of your favourite chilli oil
juice of ½ lemon
small bunch of basil, leaves picked (this would also be great with chives or parsley, or even no herbs)
1 tablespoon extra virgin olive oil
sea salt and freshly ground black pepper

Tear the mozzarella into a bowl, then dollop in the crème fraîche. Stir together, then set aside. As it sits, the two ingredients become one, creating something really delicious and creamy that is a lot like burrata.

Put the tomatoes into a bowl with a big pinch of salt (being careful not to over-salt if your chilli oil is salty) and chilli oil. Set aside for 10 minutes. This is the key to a delicious tomato. The salt will draw out the moisture from the tomatoes and bring out the flavour, and the liquid will make a dressing.

After 10 minutes, add the lemon juice and basil leaves and toss everything together.

Spoon the mozzarella mixture onto a plate or platter, then pile on the tomatoes. Finish with the oil, a little more salt and some black pepper.

# Pork and Sage Ragù

This could be one of my favourite things to eat. There's just something about the silky, scoopable retro-ness of it. As well as eating it with pasta, I also like to serve this on a puddle of quick-cook polenta and crispy sage, or just simply with some greens.

**Serves 4 generously**

2 tablespoons vegetable or olive oil, plus extra as needed
1 tablespoon fennel seeds
400 g (14 oz) minced (ground) pork or sausage meat
2 garlic cloves, grated
6–10 sage leaves, plus extra to serve
½ teaspoon chilli (hot pepper) flakes, plus extra to serve
2 celery sticks, thinly sliced
1 large fennel bulb, leek or onion
150 ml (5 fl oz/scant ⅔ cup) dry white wine
400 ml (14 fl oz/generous 1½ cups) whole (full-fat) milk
1 x 400 g (14 oz) tin of brown lentils
3 tablespoons extra virgin olive oil
350 g (12 oz) pasta (I like using small pasta shapes for spoonability reasons, but use any you have)
sea salt and freshly ground black pepper

**To serve**
grated Parmesan
lemon zest
chopped parsley

Heat the vegetable or olive oil in a heavy-based saucepan over a medium high-heat. Once the oil is shimmering hot, add the fennel seeds and fry for 30 seconds, then add the minced pork, breaking it up into small pieces with a wooden spoon. Fry for 6–8 minutes until lightly golden all over and starting to crisp up. Feel free to add a little more oil if needed. Add the garlic, sage leaves and chilli flakes and fry for a further 2 minutes until the garlic is softened and very lightly golden.

Scoop out the pork and garlic onto a plate, leaving any excess fat or oil in the pan. If there isn't any oil left, add another 2 tablespoons, then add the celery and fennel. Fry for 8–10 minutes until soft but not coloured. Return the pork to the pan, then pour in the wine and allow to bubble for 2–3 minutes before adding in the milk. Stir everything together, then cover with a lid and simmer over a low heat for 45 minutes. The milk will split, but this is good – just stir it occasionally.

After 45 minutes, add the lentils with their juices, then continue to simmer for a further 10 minutes until the sauce thickens. Taste and season as needed.

Heat the extra virgin olive oil in a small frying pan (skillet) over a medium-high heat, then add a small handful of sage leaves, along with a pinch of chilli flakes. Swirl the pan, letting the oil coat the sage leaves, and fry for 1 minute until the sage leaves crisp up. Remove from the heat and pour into a bowl.

Cook the pasta in a large saucepan of salted boiling water according to the packet instructions. Drain, reserving half a mugful of the pasta water, then stir the pasta and pasta water into the ragu and toss to coat. Serve with a generous grating of Parmesan, the crispy sage leaves, lemon zest and a little chopped parsley.

*(Images overleaf)*

# Tahini, Honey and Lemon Posset

Possets have a bit of a bad reputation, but I think they're a great, easy dessert that can be served all year round. I always seem to have a little bit of cream, yoghurt or crème fraîche left in the refrigerator, some kind of sugar and a pile of lemons or limes, so a posset is the perfect way to use up the ends of the pots. You can even make just one or two if you like. Try and get a tahini that is silky, creamy and not separated. If you have a layer of oil on the top (this happens if it's not been used for a while), just give it a really good shake or stir until smooth. This is important as you don't want a lumpy posset. These possets are great served with the shortbread on pages 182–83.

## Serves 6

400 ml (14 fl oz/generous
    1½ cups) double (heavy) cream
100 g (3½ oz/generous ½ cup)
    light brown soft sugar (this also
    works with caster/superfine
    sugar or even muscovado)
zest and juice of 3 lemons or
    4 limes (or a mixture of the two –
    you'll need about 75 ml/
    2½ fl oz/5 tablespoons juice)
pinch of sea salt
200 ml (7 fl oz/scant 1 cup) plain
    yoghurt, crème fraîche or more
    double cream
2 tablespoons honey
4 tablespoons tahini

### To serve (optional)
150 g (5½ oz) strawberries,
    raspberries or blackberries,
    roughly chopped
1 heaped tablespoon caster
    (superfine) sugar
zest and juice of 1 lemon

Pour the cream and sugar into a saucepan over a medium-high heat and bring to a steady boil, then reduce to a simmer and cook, stirring continuously so it doesn't catch on the bottom of the pan, for 5 minutes until starting to thicken. Remove from the heat and stir in the lemon zest, juice and salt, then stir in the crème fraîche, honey and tahini until thick and creamy.

Pour the mixture into six glasses, espresso cups or ramekins or into a large bowl and refrigerate for a least 4 hours, or ideally overnight.

When you're almost ready to serve, combine the berries, sugar and lemon zest and juice in a bowl. Give it a good mix, then set aside for 10 minutes (you can make these up to 2 hours in advance – the longer you leave them, the juicer they will get).

Serve the possets or posset with the berries and let everyone help themselves.

# The Easiest
# Hob Malt
# Rice Pudding

My mum used to make me rice pudding for most of my birthdays, even though I think only my dad and I like it (I especially love the skin). A scoop of baked rice pudding with some strawberry jam, fresh strawberries and a little double (heavy) cream is one of the best things, but sometimes I just don't have the patience, nor the will to rack up my energy bills, for 2 hours of cooking in the oven. So, here is my hob (stovetop) rice pudding. I've added Horlicks because it makes the rice pudding taste like the inside of a Malteser…but feel free to leave it out and use some vanilla extract or vanilla bean paste instead.

**Serves 4**

800 ml (27 fl oz/3⅓ cups)
   whole (full-fat) milk
100 ml (3½ fl oz/scant ½ cup)
   double (heavy) cream, plus extra
   to serve
125 g (4½ oz/generous ⅔ cup)
   short-grain pudding rice
4 tablespoons malted milk drink,
   such as Horlicks or Ovaltine
1 tablespoon caster sugar
   (superfine) or honey

**To serve**
200 g (7 oz) cherries, pitted
dark brown soft sugar
dark chocolate

Combine all the ingredients in a saucepan, stir, then bring to the boil, stirring regularly. This can take up to 5 minutes. As soon as it starts to boil, reduce to a very low simmer, cover with a lid and cook over a low heat for 30 minutes, stirring regularly. The rice should be soft and the mixture thickened and creamy (it will continue to thicken as it cools, too).

Serve with the cherries, a sprinkle of brown sugar, a grating of dark chocolate and a drizzle of double cream.

# EGGS

# MAYONNAISE AND AIOLI

Cambridge Sauce (page 160) on boiled asparagus

Paprika Aioli (page 158) with Roast Chicken (pages 88–89)

Créme Fraîche, Dill and Lemon Aioli (page 160) on toast with salmon and pickles

Sweetcorn Aioli (page 160)

Warm Caesar (page 162), but cold!

Lemon, Garlic, Thyme and Chilli Aioli (page 160)

# MAYONNAISE AND AIOLI

The age-old question: what's the difference between aioli and mayonnaise? Well, aioli is made with garlic and olive oil, whereas mayonnaise is made withoutout garlic and purely with a neutral oil. So really you can go both ways with this recipe by simply omitting the garlic and just using 450ml (15¼ fl oz/scant 2 cups) neutral oil to make a simple mayonnaise. The difference in method is small but I think the difference in taste is big.

Most things taste better with a dollop of homemade mayonnaise or aioli (and yes, it is different to a dollop of mayonnaise from a jar, although there's a time and place for that, too). Learn to make it and your food will be forever grateful. It's also incredibly easy to customise with different additions.

I've provided a method for making by hand and in a food processor – the latter is easier, but there's something undeniably satisfying about making it by hand (and, you never know when you'll need aioli when a food processor is not at available!). For either of the methods, if your aioli splits, don't worry! Whisk or pulse in 1 teaspoon boiling water at a time until you have a smooth mixture again. Alternatively, whisk an egg yolk in a new, clean bowl, then slowly add the split mixture to the new egg yolk until it thickens again.

## Makes 1 x medium jar

2 medium or large egg yolks
1 teaspoon Dijon mustard
1 teaspoon white wine, apple cider or red wine vinegar
½ small garlic clove, grated or finely chopped
pinch of sea salt
150 ml (5 fl oz/scant ⅔ cup) extra virgin olive oil
300 ml (10 fl oz/1¼ cups) neutral oil, such as light olive oil, rapeseed oil or vegetable oil
lemon juice, to taste
few grinds of freshly ground black pepper

## By hand

Put the egg yolks, mustard, vinegar, garlic and salt into a bowl, then place the bowl on a dish towel so the bowl doesn't slip around when whisking. Combine the two oils in a jug (pitcher).

Whisk the eggs vigorously until pale, then drizzle in the oil very slowly until the mixture starts to emulsify and thicken. Keep adding the oil until you have a thick-looking mayonnaise, bearing in mind you might not use all the oil. Squeeze in the lemon juice and check for seasoning, adjusting as necessary.

## In a food processor

Put the egg yolks, mustard, vinegar, garlic and salt into a blender and blend until pale. It's important to make sure the yolk mixture is properly mixed before adding the oil.

Combine the two oils in a jug (pitcher).

With the motor running, drizzle in the oil very slowly until the mixture starts to emulsify and thicken. Keep slowly adding the oil until you have a thick-looking mayonnaise. You might not need all the oil. Squeeze in the lemon juice and check for seasoning, adjusting as necessary.

# Aioli Variations

## Cambridge sauce

Boil 2 eggs for 8 minutes, then roughly chop along with 2 tablespoons drained capers, a few anchovies, a small handful of tarragon leaves, parsley leaves and chives. Stir into the aioli with a pinch of smoked paprika, then loosen with white wine vinegar. Serve on top of green vegetables, potatoes or even just toast with an extra sprinkling of paprika. Serve with a pile of green vegetables such as asparsgus, green beans or broccoli. Or this is also perfect in a sandwich.

## Crème fraîche, dill and lemon

Add the dill at the end and blitz until smooth, then stir in 2 tablespoons crème fraîche and some lemon zest. Best served with fish.

## Basil and caper

Finely chop a small handful of basil leaves and 2 tablespoons drained capers, then stir or blend into the aioli with 1 tablespoon caper brine. I love this served in a sandwich or dolloped on top of boiled or crispy potatoes.

## Lemon, garlic, thyme and chilli

In a small saucepan over a medium heat, combine 3 tablespoons olive oil with 2 finely sliced garlic cloves, 2 sprigs of thyme and a pinch of chilli flakes. Gently simmer for 2 minutes until the garlic is lightly golden. Allow to cool for 5 minutes, then whisk into the aioli, along with the juice and zest of half a lemon. I'd serve this tossed through some crabmeat, or just alongside some chips for dipping.

## Paprika, parsley and garlic

Very finely chop a small handful of parsley leaves, then blend or mix into the aioli. In a small saucepan over a medium heat, melt a knob of butter (about 20 g/¾ oz) with 2 tablespoons olive oil. Add 2 grated garlic cloves and 1 teaspoon paprika and gently simmer for 2 minutes. Allow to cool for 5 minutes, then whisk into the aioli, leaving a little for pouring over. This was born to be served with prawns.

## Turmeric, lime, garlic, chilli and coriander

Finely chop a small handful of coriander (cilantro) leaves, 1 red chilli and 1 garlic clove and blend or mix them into the aioli with 1 teaspoon ground turmeric and the zest and juice of 1 lime. I love this one with a fishcake or just some simply cooked vegetables, chicken or fish.

## Harissa

Mix 1–2 tablespoons of harissa paste into the aioli.

## Saffron

Melt a knob of butter (about 20 g/¾ oz) with a small pinch of saffron in a small saucepan over a medium heat or in the microwave. Allow to cool for 5 minutes, then pour into the aioli along with an extra squeeze of lemon juice. I've served this on top of a fish stew many times, but it would also be great alongside some crispy pan-fried fish and rice.

## • Curry powder and lime

In a small saucepan over a medium heat, melt a knob of butter (about 20 g/¾ oz) with 1 tablespoon curry powder until foaming and fragrant. Allow to cool for 5 minutes, then blend or mix into the aioli with the juice and zest of 1 lime. This is the perfect partner for the schnitzel on page 119.

## • Parmesan and black pepper

Grate 20 g (¾ oz) Parmesan into the aioli along with about 15 grinds of black pepper and mix well. Dipping toasted bread into this is best way to go, but again, it's heaven in a sandwich or on the side of a plain roast chicken with chips and a salad.

## • Sweetcorn

In a small pan over a medium heat, add 30 g (1 oz) butter to a small pan. Once melted add 1 grated garlic clove to cook for a minute, then add 200 g (7 oz) frozen sweetcorn or 1 fresh corn on the cob, kernels removed, swirling it into the butter to coat. For frozen, cook for 1–2 minutes until plump and yellow. For fresh, cook in the butter for 3–4 minutes until just cooked, plump and yellow.

Spoon half of the corn into the aioli and either blitz into the aioli, or just stir in if doing by hand. Dollop into a bowl, then top with the remaining corn followed by the chili flakes and black pepper to finish.

# Warm Caesar

My preference is spring greens (collard greens) here, but any leafy green would work, such as Savoy cabbage, hispi (pointed) cabbage, kale, green beans, cavolo nero (lacinato kale) or broccoli. Use whatever is in season.

I also love this with the Crispy Breadcrumbs on page 114 instead of croutons. And I HIGHLY recommend using a dollop of flavoured Aoili, especially the sweetcorn one (page 161).

**Serves 2**

2 thick slices of sourdough or
   a chunk of bread (about
   200 g/7 oz), torn in to 1 cm
   (½ inch) pieces
3 tablespoons olive oil
2–4 eggs
250 g (9 oz) spring greens
   (collard greens) or cavolo nero
   (lacinato kale), stalk removed
small handful of soft herbs, such
   as parsley, chives, mint, etc.
½ x 30 g (1 oz) tin of anchovy
   fillets (or however many you like;
   optional)
pinch of chilli (hot pepper) flakes
   (optional)
sea salt and freshly ground
   black pepper

**For the dressing**

2 tablespoons Aioli (see
   page 158) or good-quality
   shop-bought mayonnaise
zest and juice of 1 lemon
1 teaspoon Dijon mustard
50 g (1¾ oz) Parmesan, grated,
plus extra for the croutons
3 tablespoons good-quality
   extra virgin olive oil, plus extra
   to serve

Preheat the oven to 190°C fan (400°F).

Put the bread into a roasting tin with the olive oil and a pinch of salt and pepper. Grate over a little Parmesan, then toss everything with your hands until evenly combined. Roast in the oven for 10–15 minutes until golden and crisp.

Next, make the dressing. In a large bowl, whisk together the dressing ingredients, season well, then taste and add more of anything you want. I like mine lemony and mustardy, so I sometimes chuck in a little more of those. Add a tablespoon of water or so to loosen to your liking.

Bring a large saucepan of water to the boil. Boil the eggs for 6½ minutes, then remove the eggs and refresh under cold water, but keep the pan of hot water.

Add 1 teaspoon salt to the pan of water and bring back to the boil. Cook the greens for about 3 minutes, or until just cooked and bright green, then drain and toss in the Caesar dressing. Add the herbs, then grate over some extra Parmesan, drape over the anchovies and sprinkle over the chilli flakes, if using, and finish with a little more extra virgin olive oil. Serve immediately.

# Egg and Pickle

This is really the epitome of a fridge raid lunch that you'll make again and again. The classic egg mayo sandwich with extra pickle. Very very good with a slice of good quality ham too.

The butter is definitely not essential but I really recommend it. You're going to butter the bread anyway....so why not melt it and pour it over instead.

**Serves 2**

4 eggs
2 tablespoons good-quality
  mayonnaise or Aioli (see
  page 158)
1 teaspoon Dijon mustard
5 cornichons or 2 large gherkins
  (dill pickles), roughly chopped
  (or 2 tablespoons drained
  capers or green olives)
1 tablespoon pickled jalapeños,
  finely chopped
zest of 1 lemon, plus extra
  to serve
15 g (½ oz) dill, chives and
  parsley leaves, roughly chopped
10 g (½ oz) butter, melted
toasted crumpets or bread,
  to serve

First, boil the eggs in a small saucepan of boiling water for 7 minutes, then drain and refresh under cold water.

In a bowl, combine the mayonnaise, mustard, cornichons or gherkins, jalapeños, lemon zest, half the herbs and the melted butter along with a good pinch of salt and pepper. Mix well, then peel and quarter the eggs and gently stir them in.

Sccop onto toasted crumpets or bread to serve.

# Tomatoes, Eggs, Crispy Herbs

The famous sage fried eggs that everyone (including me) loves. But I'll say something potentially controversial…I don't love fried eggs. I like the crispy edges, I like the act of making them, but sometimes I just want the creaminess of an egg like this. Soft and pillowy, halfway between an omelette and scrambled eggs. By frying the herbs in the pan first, it means the eggs are then cooked in the herby flavours. So even if you just make the eggs and herbs on toast, I'd be happy.

I've used a mix of butter and olive oil, which I think some people may judge. But it's my love of Spanish and English/French cooking together. The tomatoes need the peppery extra virgin olive oil, and the eggs and herbs need the creamy, salty butter. I couldn't face removing one, but if you'd like, you can, of course, just use one or the other.

**Serves 2**

2 large tomatoes or 200 g (7 oz) cherry tomatoes, ideally the best summer can give you
1 tablespoon extra olive oil, plus extra for the tomatoes
juice of ½ lemon or 1 tablespoon red wine vinegar
knob of salted butter (around 25 g/1 oz)
a selection or all of any of the following: sage, thyme, fresh oregano, rosemary
4 eggs
sea salt and freshly ground black pepper

**To serve**
slices of toast

Start by chopping the tomatoes into rough 2 cm (¾ in) chunks (or halves and quarters if cherry tomatoes), then tip into a bowl with a big pinch of salt, a generous amount of freshly ground black pepper, a small glug of extra virgin olive oil and the lemon juice. Stir and allow to rest for at least 15 minutes (it's well worth doing to get the best flavour).

In a medium non-stick frying pan (skillet), add the butter with 1 tablespoon olive oil. Once the butter starts to foam, add the herbs and swirl the pan so the butter and oil coat the herbs. Fry for 2–3 minutes, then scoop out onto a plate, leaving half the melted butter in the pan.

Heavily whisk the eggs with a pinch of flaky sea salt in a bowl. In the same pan as you cooked the crispy herbs, add a little more butter if needed. Once the butter is foaming and melted, add the eggs. Swirl the eggs around the pan, then with a wooden spoon or spatula, drag the eggs into the middle of the pan, then lift the pan and let the runny eggs fall into the empty space. Continue around the pan so all the runny egg is gone and you have a rippled, glossy just-cooked egg omelette.

Spoon the tomatoes onto plates with some of the juices at the bottom of the bowl. Split the omelette in half with the back of the spoon, then slide each half onto a plate and top with the crispy herbs.

Scoop on toast and enjoy everything dripping down your chin, or just eat as is. I've had this with breadcrumbs from page 114 as a dinner.

# Flourless Chocolate Cake

I wrote this recipe a long time ago, and it comes out a lot for birthdays and dinners because it's pretty foolproof. You can easily swap round the types of sugar and use more caster (superfine) sugar than light brown soft sugar if that's what you have, or use all one type.

**Serves 2**

200 g (7 oz) 70% dark (bittersweet) chocolate, chopped
200 g (7 oz) unsalted butter, cut into pieces roughly the same size as the chocolate, plus extra for greasing
200 g (7 oz/1 cup) light brown soft sugar
6 eggs (room temperature), separated
35 g (1¼ oz/⅓ cup) ground almonds (almond meal) or plain (all-purpose) flour if you don't need it to be gluten-free
pinch of flaky sea salt
75 g (2½ oz) caster (superfine) sugar
seasonal berries, to serve

**Tahini cream (optional)**

300 ml (10 fl oz/1¼ cups) double (heavy) cream
3 tablespoons tahini
1 tablespoon maple syrup

Preheat the oven to 170°C fan (375°F). Grease and line a 23 cm (9 inch) cake tin (pan) with baking parchment.

Combine the chocolate and butter in a heatproof bowl set over a saucepan containing 4 cm (1½ inches) of barely simmering water. Make sure the bowl isn't touching the water. Stir until just melted, then remove from the heat and allow to cool slightly.

Once cooled a little, whisk in the light brown soft sugar, then the egg yolks one at a time, followed by the ground almonds and salt. If the chocolate splits, don't worry! Stir in 1 teaspoon boiling water at a time until you have a smooth, silky mixture.

Using a stand mixer or hand-held electric whisk, whisk the egg whites until they form stiff peaks, then gradually add the caster sugar, whisking until the egg whites form soft peaks, like a very light meringue.

Very carefully fold the meringue mixture into the chocolate, working delicately with a spatula or metal spoon until it's all evenly combined.

Carefully pour the mixture into the prepared tin, making sure not to knock out the air. Sprinkle over a little more flaky salt, then bake in the oven for 20–25 minutes. The middle should be a little gooey and the surface a bit cracked.

For the tahini cream, lightly whisk the cream in a large bowl until you have very light peaks. Stir in the tahini and give a few more whisks. Set aside while the cake bakes.

Remove the cake from the oven and allow to cool. It'll dip a little when it cools. Slice and serve with a dollop of the tahini cream and fresh berries, if using.

# Brown Sugar Custard with Biscuit Crumb

In the UK, we have a love for custard, and this is a really simple custard recipe. It's served with a lazy crunchy crumb and whatever fruit you like. I've used Lotus Biscoff biscuits (cookies) here because they are one of the best biscuits in the game, but you can use your favourite or whatever is in your cupboard. This recipe is very customisable and is always a hit with friends and family. I've served mine with the roast plums from pages 182–83, but in the height of summer I would serve it with some berries, or my personal favourite, gooseberries! This is also really good with the breadcrumb and sesame mix from page 122. Freeze any leftovers in a small container for ice cream.

## Serves 4

2 large egg yolks
20 g (¾ oz/scant ⅛ cup ) light or dark muscovado sugar
1 tablespoon honey (or 5 g/ ¼ oz more brown sugar)
1 heaped teaspoon cornflour (cornstarch)
350ml (12 fl oz/1½ cups) whole milk
100 ml (3½ fl oz/scant ½ cup) double (heavy) cream
pinch of sea salt
poached or roasted fruit (see pages 182–83) or berries

### For the biscuit crumb

50 g (1¾ oz/⅓ cup) nuts of choice, such as flaked (slivered) almonds, hazelnuts or pecans
6 biscuits (cookies) of choice (I like Lotus Biscoff or digestives/graham crackers, but ginger nuts/snaps would also be great), crushed
pinch of flaky sea salt

First, toast the nuts for the crumb in a wide frying pan (skillet) over a medium heat for a few minutes until lightly golden, then remove from the heat and allow to cool. Alternatively, you can toast the nuts on a baking tray (pan) in the oven at 180°C fan (400°F) for 8 minutes. Once cooled, roughly chop the nuts.

Combine the nuts in a bowl with the crushed biscuits and salt, then set aside.

In a large bowl, lightly whisk the egg yolks, brown sugar, honey and cornflour together.

Bring the milk and cream to a gentle boil in a small non-stick saucepan, then remove from the heat and very slowly pour into the egg mixture, whisking as you pour so the egg doesn't scramble.

Now pour the mixture back into the saucepan. Stir continuously over a low heat for 6–8 minutes until the mixture thickens enough to coat the back of a wooden spoon. Do not let it boil as this will scramble the custard, so be patient! Stir in the salt, then remove from the heat.

Serve the custard with the roasted fruit and biscuit crumble.

# FRUIT

ANY CAKE CAKE CAKE

Any Cake Cake (pages 176–77) as a lemon drizzle loaf cake

Any Cake Cake (pages 176–77) as a cupcake with buttercream

Any Cake Cake (pages 176–77) baked in a round tin with cherries

Sheet Cake (pages 176–77) with whipped cream and macerated strawberries (page 181)

Any Cake Cake (pages 176–77) baked in a brownie tin with apricots and flaked (slivered) almonds

Any Cake Cake (pages 176–77), doubled up with frosting and jam

# ANY CAKE CAKE

This is essentially a cake recipe for all. It's really easy to make and can be adapted in any way you want, hopefully meaning no trips to the shop will be needed! It's a great way to use seasonal fruit, but it's also perfect for using up those bags of frozen fruit you've got hiding in the freezer or that one apple that's looking quite sad in your fruit bowl.

I've developed this recipe to be fail-safe – it should always be perfectly risen and light because of the reaction between the yoghurt, lemon juice and bicarbonate of soda (baking soda). This reaction produces carbon dioxide, which causes the cake to rise, much like soda bread (fun science fact for you!).

110 g (4 oz) unsalted butter, at room temperature, plus extra for greasing
Demerara sugar, for the tin
300 g (10½ oz/scant 2½ cups) plain (all-purpose) flour
1½ teaspoons baking powder
1 teaspoon bicarbonate of soda (baking soda)
pinch of salt
125 g (4½ oz/generous ½ cup) caster (superfine) sugar
juice of 1 lemon, plus the zest of 2 lemons if you want a more intense lemon flavour
3 medium eggs
220 g (7¾ oz) plain 5% fat yoghurt
2–4 tablespoons milk (if your yoghurt is thick set)
1 teaspoon vanilla extract or vanilla bean paste (optional but recommended)

Preheat the oven to 180°C fan (400°F). Line a 23 cm (9 inch) springform round cake tin (pan) with baking parchment or grease liberally with butter and coat with Demerara sugar.

In a large bowl, mix together the flour, baking powder, bicarbonate of soda and salt, plus any spices you want to use (see opposite).

In a separate bowl, beat together the butter, sugar and lemon zest, if using, with a hand-held electric whisk or in a stand mixer using the beater attachment until light and fluffy, stopping to scrape down the sides as you go – this should take about 3–4 minutes, but it will depend on how soft your butter is.

Add the eggs one by one, beating between each addition, until the egg is fully incorporated and the mixture is light and creamy.

Now add a quarter of the flour mixture and fold it in with a spoon, followed by a quarter of the yoghurt and lemon juice, folding again. Continue alternating additions until both are used up. The key is to not overmix! The less mixing you do, the lighter the sponge will be, so just gently fold in the ingredients until there are no more patches of yoghurt or flour. If needed, loosen with a little milk until the mixture is creamy and drops easily from a spoon.

Scrape the mixture into the prepared tin and top with your chosen fruit topping (see opposite).

## Flavour variations

3 cardamom pods, bashed open and seeds crushed or ½ teaspoon ground cardamom

zest of 2 lemons

1 teaspoon ground ginger or 2 balls of stem ginger, chopped, plus 1 tablespoon stem ginger syrup

50 g (1¾ oz) flaked (slivered) almonds, toasted, half stirred in with the flour and half sprinkled on top

## Fruit toppings

200 g (7 oz) strawberries, halved or quartered

3–4 plums, halved and stoned

100 g (3½ oz) fresh or frozen cherries (pitted if fresh)

1 cooking apple or 2 eating (dessert) apples, peeled, cored and sliced into 1 cm (½ inch) wedges

100 g (3½ oz) frozen raspberries or blackberries

Bake in the oven for 35 minutes until a skewer inserted into the centre comes out clean, then remove from the oven and allow to cool for 5 minutes before removing from the tin and placing on a wire rack to cool completely.

## Adaptable baking times

This mixture is easily adaptable for different shapes and sizes of cake tin (pan), just follow the guidelines below.

- 2 x 20 cm (8 inch) round tins for a sandwich cake: bake for 20–25 minutes at 180°C fan (400°F)

- 26 cm cake tin: bake for 30 minutes at 180°C fan (400°F)

- 12-hole muffin tin (for large muffins) or smaller 24-hole cupcake tin: bake for 15 minutes at 180°C fan (400°F)

- 30 x 20 cm (12 x 8 inch) sheet pan: bake for 30 minutes at 180°C fan (400°F)

- 900 g (2 lb) high-sided loaf tin: bake for 50–60 minutes at 160°C fan (350°F)

- 2 x 450 g (1 lb) loaf tins: bake for 40 minutes at 180°C fan (400°F)

# Layered Cake Bowl

I like baking occasionally, but in reality I can never eat a whole cake and there's always half leftover, sat in the corner not looking its best. But never, ever throw away a cake that's a bit stale! Instead, make this. If you don't have any cake left over, make one fresh – it's worth it, as serving cake like this is fun way of getting all the good bits in one scoop.

**Serves 4–6, depending on how much cake you have leftover!**

300 g (10½ oz) leftover cake of any sort or shortbread (or however much you have)

50 g (1¾oz) nuts, such as flaked (slivered) almonds, whole almonds, pecans or walnuts (or 25 g/1 oz desiccated/dried shredded coconut or toasted coconut flakes)

500 g (1 lb 2 oz) seasonal fruit of choice, such as strawberries, raspberries, blackberries, kiwis, peeled and sliced oranges, tinned mango or leftover roasted fruit (pages 182–83)

2 tablespoons caster (superfine) sugar (optional)

juice of ½ lemon (optional)

600 ml (20 fl oz/2½ cups) double (heavy) cream

200 g (7 oz) Greek yogurt, mascarpone, ricotta or crème fraîche

1 teaspoon vanilla extract or vanilla bean paste

40 g (1½ oz/scant ¼ cup) dark or light brown soft sugar

100 ml (3½ fl oz/scant ½ cup) brandy, rum or any liqueur (optional)

Preheat the oven to 180°C fan (400°F).

Wrap the cake in foil and bake it in the oven for 10–15 minutes until warmed through. Remove from the oven and allow to cool for 30 minutes, then tear into 3 cm (1¼ inch) chunks.

While the oven is hot, spread out your chosen nuts on a baking sheet and toast in the oven for 8 minutes until lightly golden, then remove and set aside to cool before finely chopping if needed.

Meanwhile, if you're using using berries, combine them with the sugar and lemon juice in a bowl. Stir and set aside to macerate and create a delicious juice.

Very lightly whip the cream with the yoghurt, mascarpone, crème fraîche or ricotta and vanilla – you should just be able to make trails in the cream mix. You want it more runny than thick here, so if you over-whip it, don't panic, just pour in a little more cream and stir by hand until you're happy with the texture.

Pour your chosen alcohol, if using, into a bowl, then lightly dip in the cake chunks until just coated but not soggy.

To assemble, put the cake chunks into a large bowl, then top with a layer of the fruit, then a layer of cream and then a sprinkling of sugar. Repeat until you've used everything up, finishing with cream, a little more fruit and the toasted nuts. Serve immediately.

# Kitty's Shortbread to go with any fruit

I've been making this shortbread for as long as I can remember. It is the first thing I could ever make well, and I've made it thousands of times. I actually had to work out how to make it using grams, as I learnt the recipe in ounces (the rule is 2/4/6: 2 oz sugar, 4 oz butter and 6 oz flour – or you can do 4/8/12 if you want extra for snacking on and to give to neighbours). The shortbread used to be served with my mum's chocolate nemesis cake at my parents' restaurant and was one of the things on the menu that never changed, for good reason. It's by no means a genius recipe, but it goes with absolutely anything. My dad's favourite way to eat it is simply with fresh raspberries and cream, and eating it this way reminds me of long, English summer Sunday lunches in the garden, which would end with us all falling asleep on the grass around the table. Here, I'm serving it with spiced, roasted fruit and softly whipped cream.

You can easily turn this recipe into a crumble by adding 50 g (1¾ oz/½ cup) oats to the shortbread mixture and loosely spreading it over the fruit mixture before baking.

## Serves 6–8

6 plums (or cherries, rhubarb, apples, pears or strawberries, or a mixture), halved and stoned
zest of 1 lemon, orange or lime, plus juice of ½
2 tablespoons water
spices of choice, such as 1 cinnamon stick, 1 vanilla pod or 2 cardamom pods
25 g (1 oz/2 tablespoons) light brown soft sugar or caster (superfine) sugar
200 ml (7 fl oz/scant 1 cup) double (heavy) cream, to serve
200 g (7 oz) yoghurt, to serve

Preheat the oven to 180°C fan (400°F) and line a 24 cm (9½ inch) round cake or tart tin (pan) or a 20 x 30 cm (8 x 12 inch) brownie tin with baking parchment. You can also bake the shortbread in a 20 cm (8 inch) round tin and bake it for 30 minutes. It will be thicker, but some people prefer it like this, so go with whatever you like.

To make the shortbread, put all the ingredients into a food processor. Make sure the butter is really cold, as this is what will ensure the shortbread is crisp and crumbly. If it's a bit soft, cube the butter and then freeze it briefly. Pulse the ingredients a few times until the mix resembles breadcrumbs. If you don't have a food processor, use your fingers to rub the butter into the other ingredients.

Tip the mixture into the prepared tin and pat it down evenly (a good way to do with is with bottom of a glass, pressing down the mixture until you have a flat and compressed surface). Refrigerate for at least 30 minutes, or up to 4 days if you want to make it ahead.

## For the shortbread

55 g (2 oz/¼ cup) caster
(superfine) sugar, plus extra for
sprinkling
120 g (4¼ oz) cold unsalted
butter, cubed
165 g (6 oz/1⅓ cups) plain
(all-purpose) flour
pinch of sea salt

Bake the chilled shortbread in the oven for 25 minutes until very lightly golden, then remove from the oven and sprinkle with a little extra caster sugar before slicing into 6–8 pieces while it's warm. Allow to cool in the tin for at least 20 minutes.

Meanwhile, put the plums (or other fruit) into a 20 cm (8 inch) square roasting tin (you want it to be just big enough to fit your fruit snugly). Add the citrus zest and juice along with the water, spices and sugar. Give everything a good mix, then cover with foil and roast in the oven for 30–40 minutes until the juices are bubbling and the fruit is tender but not falling apart (roast for 20 minutes if using cherries or rhubarb, or if your fruit is particularly ripe).

Very lightly whip the cream and stir in the yoghurt. Serve the fruit, shortbread and cream at the table so everyone can help themselves.

# Brown-sugar Crusted Fool with Lime-macerated Berries

This is my childhood! Best served with any seasonal fruit plus the shortbread from pages 182–3, which is my Mum's most famous dessert. People are always so impressed when it's served to the table with the dark brown sugar top (do not skip this part!), as it melts on to the cream and becomes a sort of caramel.

The mix of yogurt and cream makes it mousse-like, meaning each spoonful feels so light. It's the most simple thing to make in the book and one of my favourites.

**Serves 4**

300 ml (10 fl oz/1¼ cups) double (heavy) cream
400 g (14 oz) Greek or plain yoghurt
3 tablespoons dark brown soft sugar, plus extra to serve
250 g (9 oz) strawberries, raspberries or blackberries (quartered if using strawberries)
zest and juice of 2 limes
2 tablespoons caster (superfine) sugar

Whip the double cream until you can just start to see that it's thickening up, then fold through the yoghurt and spoon into a bowl. Sprinkle over the brown sugar, then set aside in the refrigerator. The sugar will melt onto the creamy mixture and create a caramel-like top.

In a bowl, combine the berries with the lime zest and juice and caster sugar, then set aside to macerate for 5 minutes, or up to 1 hour.

Either serve separately at the table for people to help themselves or layer into glasses, finishing with the cream and an extra sprinkle of brown sugar.

# INDEX

# ACKNOWLEDGEMENTS

Acknowledgements are such a strange one for me to write because they are the first thing I look at in a cookbook. It's a big team effort and although I did the food, props and wrote it, there is so much other work that goes into making a cookbook. A small thank you goes a long way.

These will be too long, but I want to thank so many people for helping with this.

Issy Croker, you already know how grateful I am for going above and beyond to get everything shot for this book (note to self – shooting numerous versions for most recipes is A LOT of work and I'm so sorry I put you through the chaos of getting them done). I owe you…Issy and I met on a cookbook shoot 7 years ago and I really did love her from the get go. You've helped me through so many things and are always there when I need you. You're my favourite person to cook with. We love everything from the food shopping, to the planning, the wild ideas, and the cooking. You have a flair for hosting and I love how much we love it together. Let's host and cook together forever.

Clare, you sent me the most gorgeous Instagram message 4 years ago and I'm so happy that, for once, I replied. We've gone on some wild trips and jobs and its been so fun to have you around to see the funny side of things. Thank you for helping me on this when I thought I was going mad, you always make me feel better.

Poppy, thank you so much for coming to help – I don't know what I would have done without you! You work so hard, always look so glamorous and always have a smile on your face.

Georgia, I'm half sorry and half grateful I roped you into this mad world of cookbooks, but since we met a few years ago you've really come into your own. Thank you so much for stepping in and saving the day. You are a ray of sunshine and nothing is ever a problem.

Issy G-P – my lovely publisher. Thank you for putting up with my lack of replies…I think it helps that you know I'm on other peoples' shoots (mostly with you!) and am physically unable to reply. But I still feel terrible! We've been on so many mad jobs together that I kind of hope this has been an easier one for you. Thank you so much for everything and for getting me over the finish line.

Lizzie Mayson, you stepped in at the last minute to get some extra shots for me to fill some gaps. Poor Issy G-P emailing me, 'If you're going to do them…. we need these images…like…last week.' Lizzie, you went above and beyond to help me and I don't know how to express my gratitude or love for you. I've never met a more infectious person than Lizzie. Every time we are together I leave feeling amazing. You make me laugh the most and I just want to spend the rest of my life in corners of restaurants and bars drinking, eating and laughing with you. Thank you for being my podcast voice note friend – my mornings are the best when I wake up to '10-minute voice note from Lizzie'.

Florence and El – thank you for testing my recipes. You are two people I trust the most with testing and I couldn't have done it without you.

Luke – I'm a tough one to please with design because I have such a clear vision but you've really taken everything I said and made it better.

To Melissa Hemsley. I wouldn't have got anywhere without you. We met on a shoot nearly 10 years ago and walked to the tube together, and have been close friends ever since. You are the most kind, generous and mad person. The only person I know who would travel hours just to see a friend for 10 minutes. I can't express enough how much you mean to me.

Andrew – my kind and patient boyfriend. Thank you for purely being you – for putting up with the constant tapping on the laptop, the tearful calls, the stress, the washing up and the doubts. You always know what to say, and are always so calm, so reassuring and supportive. I am a person who does what they want, when they want, and tells no one my plans. You're so good at just letting me be, but also being there when I really need you. I love you, Love.

I nearly forgot to thank my family...! Mainly my blonde hair, blue-eyed clever sister Lily, who let me come and cook at her house, make a mess and then leave. I hope the months of a filled fridge and fun weekends with me was worth it! I'm very grateful for your support in my chaotic life. Also – Lily can cook too!

Dora, my brown-haired, tall, farm girl middle sister, who has just had the most perfect baby girl Sydney. Dora is a very good taste tester – although she's very easy to please and will eat a whole jar of herrings as a snack. But either way, she seems to think everything I make is delicious, so I'll take that.

Thank you to my parents, who taught me so much about food. My upbringing so intensely revolved around food, and I never realised how much I knew until I was older and found that not everyone could make a whole Sunday roast from the age of 12?!

# ABOUT KITTY

London, Mallorca and Dublin-based food writer, food stylist and prop stylist Kitty Coles tells stories through food with her immediately recognisable relaxed, lived-in style. She has worked on many cookbooks over the last 10 years of her career, including books by Anna Jones, Joe Wicks, Gennaro Contaldo, Pasta Grannies, Ixta Belfrage, Thomasina Miers, Melissa Hemsley and Hugh Fearnley-Whittingstall, and she regularly styles for publications such as *The Guardian* and *The Telegraph*.

Kitty grew up cooking in her family's restaurant with a daily-changing chalkboard menu, learning about flavours and using seasonal produce. She's the second generation of family restaurants and catering, so food and eating around the table has always been the focus of her upbringing.

Her dad grew up in Mallorca, so her food has a Mediterranean influence and she has an ethos for cooking simply and making things go a long way.

Inspired by many chefs and cooks she has worked with over the years, Kitty focuses on simple ingredients, cooked with minimal effort and time to create maximum flavours in any kitchen.